Published internati…
44 Rays of Sunshin…

Cover image by the artist Sam Cannon

http://www.samcannonart.co.uk.

This book is for my mother, without whose unwavering love I would not be here today; and for the three wise men: my father, my grandfather, and my love - each of whom has changed my life.

But most of all this book is for you, whoever you are, so that you too might give direction when those around you are floundering.

44 - The owl flew into the field so early one morning that the girl was still dreaming. And the bird said to her this is the beginning of your new life. The girl nodded her head as if she understood and promised herself that everything would be different.

'Stop here. This is the place' by Susan Conley

Introduction

Let's begin with me.

I have always been an over-thinker; deeper than the average puddle, you might say. It has made forming relationships a complicated affair and, truthfully, I've never been very good at them. Apart from with my parents, that is, though I would later realise that this was a given. I never had to question their love for me, it was just there, unconditionally.

My name is Lucy. I probably should have mentioned that first, but then I do tend to put the thinking before the practicalities. I am 5'6", blond and leggy with a suitably large bust, and... ok, so that's not quite true. I'm more dirty blonde, small bust, pretty average looking and now, at the age of 37, floating around somewhere in the middle of my life.

My relationships with men would be a psychologist's dream. Whilst I had an idyllic upbringing that should have meant for simple and easy relationship building, that overly-thinking mind of mine would always get the better of me. So, after several failed relationships and sailing into my late twenties, I went to visit my parents and declared to them that I was done. I was done trying. That actually relationships made me feel unhappy, so there would be no wedding, no grandchildren, and it would forever be at their door that I would call for my love and reassurance, which every human requires. As usual, their response was one of unquestioned acceptance and my Dad - being Dad - talked to me about the trials and tribulations of love. He had given me Kahil Gibran's book, *The Prophet*, for my sixteenth birthday. In it, he states that, 'if you are not to experience love's sadness then you must also excuse yourself of its amazing and wondrous highs', or words to that effect. I was ok with that. I was ok with accepting the level playing field of love and emotion. I'd take what my parents and grandad had to offer me and be grateful for the uncomplicated and unconditional love they could provide.

After that day of epiphany (that I had relayed to my parents) I felt lighter somehow, lighter of the personal pressure that I had put onto myself to not feel on edge in every relationship I attempted to have. Somehow, by accepting that I could be content without the prospect of a romantic relationship allowed me to remove it as a burden, and I was grateful to not feel bad about being happy alone.

Perhaps you are reading this thinking, doesn't she discuss these things with her friends? Of course I had friends, many of them, but I was always the single one, the one who could and would travel to them, the one to invite if they wanted a laugh and a good time, the one not to invite to a couples evening. I was the godmother to their children, the person too eager to help and be generous with time and money. I recognised this in myself but in time, as with all good things, circumstances change and what happened to me - well, it changed everything.

I had studied a management course at Leeds and had completed it at a time in my life when I was more of an actions-over-thoughts type of person. Every thought was a good one and I would jump straight in there both feet first. I was lucky, in many ways, as it all seemed to work out well for me. I would often say to my dad that, although I did have some tough times, I always felt very lucky. His response would be, "well, we make our own luck in life". He would repeatedly tell me the story of Julius Caesar, when Caesar asks his men about the recruitment of his new right hand man. He asks, "but is he lucky?" because he believed that fortune favours the brave and that a man makes his own luck. I never had reason to doubt this thought process, though my conviction has wavered from time to time.

I am lucky for many reasons: my parents met and married from university, they were well travelled, thoughtful older parents, they treated me with a sternness that showed that they cared and a humour that kept laughter at the forefront of most of our conversations, as it still does. They live in the same house I was brought up in and so I always enjoy the act of 'going back home' whenever life doesn't quite go to plan. Dad, in the winter, takes great joy in preparing a fire in the living room hearth; the bean bag that was made by my mother some 30 years prior is pulled out and a blanket put over me for comfort. Lucky is not a strong enough word for the love I feel from my parents. They always want to fix everything, fix me, and to be honest they do a pretty grand job of it. Sometimes though there are things, as we discovered, that cannot be fixed. The pot is broken and pieces are missing. It will be glued back together but it will look different and serve a different purpose.

I spent most of my time up to the age of thirty working my way up in a mindless career, that in truth served no purpose to anyone other than providing a very decent salary and allowing me a financial freedom that could then be one less worry for my overly-thinking mind. I loved achieving the next promotion or changing jobs but I had gradually come to realise that my purpose in the world didn't lie in making sure that various companies were kept warm enough, or cool enough, or were adequately stocked in two-ply toilet rolls. When my final days come this is not what I want to be remembered for. I had thought about doing so many things, doing acts of kindness for sponsorship rather than money, as I was sick of the world and my life revolving around it. I thought I might like to become a foster parent, as I thought that there was no need to have my own children when so many children need someone to take care of them. Boy, I thought about it all...

going abroad and helping, I didn't want to get to reach the end of my days for the vicar only to be able to say, 'Well, she worked hard' and then exit stage left.

Of course, I have been a walking contradiction in most areas of my life for as long as I can remember. Were someone to ask me my deepest thoughts or desires, I would state my answer whilst yearning for the complete opposite. I am independent but I expect men to be gentlemen, and to ensure that the traditional roles of women and men remain. It makes understanding myself challenging, so God help someone else who should try to. My dreams and desires have always been erratic and plentiful. They consisted of travelling the world, to helping the world - just say 'yes' to everything was my motto. It meant that by the age of thirty I had experienced a lot, more than the average person anyway, and had certainly earned more than an average amount too. I needed nothing and yet felt like I had nothing that I needed. The problem was I had no idea what it was that I actually wanted to achieve.

Being near the sea was my passion. I always felt its relevance but didn't know why, yet when sadness hit for whatever reason the sea and the sound of the waves was where I was drawn. I dreamt of living by the sea, if I could ever sit still for long enough to do it - but in saying that, I knew I would make it a reality one day. People say I'm determined, like an ox, a powerful animal of great stead and strength, and maybe that's true. But everyone is softer on the inside, with a core that can melt at the touch of a lover's hand. And that love can be a great determining force.

So that's me, and what follows is my story; the tale of what happened to me between the ages of thirty and thirty-six (ish), and how those events came to shape the person that I have become today.

Chapter One

The story of two lovers.

The passion between the lovers made for arguments, not arguments of the obsessive and controlling kind but of the intense kind, which made love grow and roots plant themselves. It became a passion so intertwined that it had no beginning and no end. Although they both knew they were meant to meet, there was a doubt in the boy, a doubt that made him wonder whether she wanted it as much as him. His attitude towards love had been so flippant at the start; how foolish of him to now find himself firmly within its grasp, with no way to backtrack on his previously dismissive stance.

Their lives came together like converging seas, thrashing intensely at the point of connection before settling into an endless stream of ripples.

Him:
We met at work and became friends because of a similar sense of humour and work ethic, which made daily conversations inevitable and, ultimately, addictive. I would often call, desperate to speak to her about her day, making some passing comment about who she had been on the phone to. I could feel something, I just didn't know what to call it. An obsession to be with her and a part of her daily routine was growing and taking over my impulses.

I knew I had to speak to her. I knew nothing more than that she made me smile and that I could make her smile, it was as simple as that. I knew I was carrying a pain from my past that I could not let go of and she made it easier in many ways, in fact it was no longer there when I was speaking with her - it would simply disappear. I had never thought much of this friendship until I had asked what she was doing one evening and she had mentioned a romantic date that she needed to prepare for. My heart sunk to unimaginable depths and suddenly a fear took over that I had not felt since I was a teenager. I realised that the feeling I had was jealousy. She consumed my mind that night, as I lay in bed with the wrong woman. I hoped that this was not the end, that her friendship and availability to talk to her was not going to diminish because of her commitment to someone else. I needed my friend and our daily chats.

How pleased I was when I called the next morning to find the date had been a disaster. I asked for all the details, What went wrong? What was he like? I was genuinely curious. It was then that I knew I had an issue that I could not change.

Her:
After realising it was time to get up and out of the work routine that was leading my life's path, I decided to get out on the dating scene and found an attractive prospect. He was a pilot, had his own teeth, full head of hair, dark and of average height. After our first date he asked to see me again, but I had struggled to find the excitement of conversation and connection that I (maybe overly optimistically) had longed for. It was

disappointing. On paper it should have worked so well, but in reality I knew that it would only be a soul connection that could ever truly take my heart.

I struggled to do much more dating after this and after several months had passed, and an opportunity to holiday with a friend had presented itself, life was pretty much the same. My friends were the same, work was the same, I had once again decided to take myself out of the dating pool; I was tired of it all, and besides, I had enough relationships with enough people on enough levels to make do without anything romantic. Anyway, I was looking forward to the last minute holiday my friend had booked as I had no idea where we would end up. I had asked my best friend at work to cover my workload, as was usual for us to do for each other because we spoke everyday so we knew each other's regions and work loads. I was waiting at the airport - well, waiting for the departure gate to come up - when he, my best friend at work, called. It wasn't unusual for him to call as we spoke daily, sometimes twice or three times, but this time he asked where I was going, told me to take care, come back safely, and when he put down the phone something had changed. I knew that something had changed but I put it to the back of my mind.

Him:
Several months later, when she went away on holiday, everything seemed to be more difficult

than before. The desire and longing to be with her was consuming and at times was overwhelming. I was unable to remove her from my mind. I instinctively went to call her every day, my fingers itching to dial her number, and so I knew I would find myself with a problem that I may not be able to resolve. My predicament felt like the heaviest weight imaginable. I was stuck in a loveless relationship that I had committed to but I had fallen for another girl - a girl who felt like the other half to complete me. So when she returned from her holiday I wanted to make her feel bad, for putting me in this predicament, for making me feel this way. I was filled with a fire of anger, frustration and jealousy at not being able to have her fully. I was confused and conflicted and I needed to push her away. It was never going to end well.

Her:
I returned to problems at work that, quite frankly, I just didn't need. The man who had become my best friend was causing problems that only my worst enemy would want to inflict upon me. It was so frustrating and hurtful, it soured the vibes of a holiday which I had so much enjoyed. It was like he was just being an absolute arse on purpose. I could not understand why he was behaving this way, it was causing me to take a serious dislike to him. If that was him aim, he was achieving it.

Him:
She stopped talking to me. Oh God, this pushing

her did not work. What did I hope to achieve? I don't even know myself. I can't be with her and can't be without her, no one to admit it to either. A week has gone by and my heart aches for this missed friendship.

Her:
What a complete arse. He has messaged me, asking if I'm still grumpy. Grrrrr, what an arse. I don't need friends like that.

Him:
I keep messaging, trying to be funny but I'm not sure it's working. I can see in my mind's eye the corners of her mouth rising, but maybe that's just wishful thinking.

Her:
He keeps messaging. After three weeks of this he's made me smile - it's time to respond. I think he's learnt his lesson, he now knows I'm not a pushover.

Him:
My relationship at home had long been over, over before it had even started. I was now putting it down to a midlife crisis, a serious misjudgement of suitability. No relationship borne of an affair will ever lead to a bed of roses. I had left my first wife to be with her, but I knew even then that it was the wrong decision. Yet while I had learnt those lessons from the past, they did nothing to help my current situation. I was scared to make the same

mistakes, too scared of what I felt to say anything, so internally paralysed by fear that all I could muster was bravado. Nonetheless, I ended up on the phone to her for hours and hours. The conversation never ending, words spilling out of us unfiltered and bare. I needed to talk to someone - no, not just someone - I needed to talk to her. I had to admit my life's mistakes, to be myself and it was only with her that could do that. I felt an overwhelming need to hear her voice all of the time; something was not just changing, it had already changed. My heart was lost in a longing to speak to her all the time. I convinced myself it was just a rebound reaction of repressed feelings, of my failures and a need to be around someone... that's what I hoped, anyway.

Her:
As I lay on the bed, he had called and I had paused the movie I was watching. The conversation went into its second hour, the phone was now having to go on charge and I thought that while I liked to talk, there weren't many people that you could talk to like this. Our conversation turned to secrets and confidences and if there had been any doubt of the change in our relationship, now was that turning point. I wasn't sure though, unconvinced that whilst there was undoubtedly a friendship there anything more was less certain. I had not been attracted to him at first, but I knew that my life would be a little duller were he not part of it, if the conversations were to stop. He had called me this day without the usual pleasantries of even

asking how I was, it seemed he didn't need niceties anymore, a clear comfort was blossoming between us. He asked, "if you went out with someone that you were getting on really well with and then they said they lived on a barge would you still like them?" Slightly aghast, I felt genuinely bemused by the conversation - why would anyone stop liking someone because of the place they live? It's like saying I will only like you if you have a certain type of car. I began a monologue of my opinions on the subject, stating that anyone worth their salt would never refuse to be with someone because of something material. I was later to discover it was a life he had been used to. He then confided in me that he had moved out of his home.

Him:
Through the conversations we had, she made me realise that my life had been so much about what I could measure: how much money, the size of my house, the area I lived in. I realised that I attracted people like that to my life, people who valued the material over all else. It was something that stayed in my mind for a long time. I felt a need to change the priorities that had become a distraction to discovering what happiness really means.

Her:
The winter months were starting to draw near. I felt fortunate to be in a modern flat which, while small, was warm, safe and cosy. The location was awesome, so quiet but a stone's throw from the town's shopping. I had a good job and felt blessed

to have so much in my life to be grateful for. I had organised the Christmas work do for the area and as it approached I was mindful that he was coming, that something had changed so much between us and I was unsure about what that would mean in the long term.

Him:
I kept thinking about her. I knew we had the work night out, I knew that there was a choice: I could keep my best friend but always have feelings for her, or I could break the safety to see what we could become if we tried. I wasn't sure I could. I feared that I would lose my best friend, in fact I knew it, but in the end I had to try.

Her:
So when he kissed me, which was not so much of a surprise to be honest, it was not a kiss that matched the bond that had been built between us. It was kind of awkward and nervous, unrehearsed like he had never kissed anyone before.

Him:
Confidence was never an issue for me, but suddenly I was completely floored and out of my comfort zone. I kissed her like it was my first kiss and in so many ways that was what it felt like. I stopped, told her I could do better than this and that kissing my best friend had not been part of the plan, but of course it had. The second attempt was perfect. I forgot all the other kisses I'd ever had, it was already like home, it was already where

I wanted to belong.

Her:
Well it got better, the kisses, the hugs and actually in truth it felt like this is how we had always been. Every kiss and touch and hand held was like our friendship on its own had never existed, that we had always been together in this bubble. That's how we spent the following two weeks, until it burst, of course.

Him:
I have had things that I had wanted in my life, I have had happiness, I have felt content within myself. But what I felt was so much stronger than what I had ever felt before, I didn't know how I knew it but I could just see it, I could see the future and it was with her. She was a future that was brighter than anything I'd had for a long time. I couldn't help but think that if I could do this with her, if she could accept me so easily for being me, then surely I could make it work with my ex, I could do that and not leave my children without a father. It is selfish to think that I could have happiness with her and knowingly leave them behind. I was torn between my devotion as a father and the overwhelming wave of love that had consumed me.

Her:
He decided to leave me after just a few weeks. But in those few weeks it had felt like we had discovered home, like we had always been

together, since forever. So when he left, I fell to the floor and wept. I wept not only for the loss of the future I knew we could have but for the best friend I had lost forever.

Him:
I knew I would lose my best friend, I knew it and still I went ahead with it. I felt so annoyed but I knew that it was not my own happiness that should come first. I could not leave knowing that my children wouldn't have a father, I couldn't continue to carry the guilt of my decisions, not again. So I sacrificed my chance of happiness with her for the knowledge that my children would have their father with them every day. I couldn't let what I thought was my selfishness in wanting to let myself fall in love with her override my love for my children and my duty to them. Guilt was weighing heavily on me, a burden I could not shift.

Her:
Everything had changed in our friendship, my safety net had gone. I was blinded by the feelings I had for him. After he broke up with me, he had wanted to see me, he'd write to me to tell me his news, how he missed me and then fail to respond once he had my attention. He had wanted our new year to be spent together and then had failed to arrive. I had believed foolishly before he kissed me that it was just a friendship, something that I could live without if I had to. I felt hurt that he had not wanted it enough, angry that our friendship could not be repaired.   I became a recluse,

unhappy in my own skin and unable to find the direction that I had previously had.

Him:
I wanted to see her, speak to her, anything to keep her near me, but the guilt would always surpass the instinct and need. I made promises and let her down so much, so I should not have been surprised when she asked me to stop contacting her, when she blocked me from her life. That day she took a piece of my heart.

Her:
Weeks turned into months. I managed to avoid him and keep my dignity. I pulled myself out of the depression and made a plan, things to do, a direction and focus. He had turned up where I was working one day, asked for a second chance, but it was too late, too late for me to risk my heart again. In time maybe we could have our friendship but I could not give it another go, not now. He had made a mistake, he had thought he could fix the past, but in trying to fix it by following his head, he was only making it worse.

Him:
By the time Spring had started, I had come to the realisation that it was not me, it was the circumstances. Of course, I did not want the children to be without a father but equally I did not want them to grow up thinking that unhappiness is a life that you accept, that people

argue and that's just the way things go. I knew it, I knew I had to do something about the unhappiness of the relationship that I had put myself back into, and so I left, even though I could not repair what I had with what I was to discover would be my greatest love.

Anyway, she rang me out of the blue and I was so happy and so angry that I had been blocked from her life - but I missed her, so I picked up. She said she missed her friend. She had been given options at work, I knew what she was asking, I knew that she had the option to be nearer to me, that we could give it a go, and even though I had asked her for this, the fear took over me once again. I could have asked her to stay, but I couldn't have committed, and I knew this would be another regret but it was safer this way. I lost my best friend and I was not worthy of the love she had given me. So she accepted a new job and moved farther away because I told her to. I had nothing but happiness for her but I was sad for myself, as I knew then that she would leave and she would want to distance herself from me even more. I had hurt her; she deserved better than what I could offer her.

Her:
So I was feeling good. The new job offer was a boost to my confidence, but when I called him to say that they'd offered me more money than advertised to go work for them he was just quiet. I had expected him to be happier for me - after all,

he was the one who'd told me to take the new opportunity! I had given him a chance, we had gone back and forth in a push and pull scenario of dancing around our feelings in the early spring, which seemed ironic, but neither of us were ready to take the leap at the same time. It was not helping either of us on our journey. I felt empowered, now I had made the choice, I was looking at new places to live and planning my move. He had seemed sad, he had his son coming to stay in the holidays, his relationship with him had been divided through his second relationship with the girlfriend, he was anxious about his imminent arrival, but I knew that he would be enough for him, it was a shame that he couldn't see that. Although he knew his son would be happy just coming to visit him - there was no need for big days out, just time with his father was all the boy needed - his fear of the childhood that he could not have given him and the guilt of those missed years was too much for him to take.

Him:
It was only her I could tell about the guilt, it was only her who did not judge me. When she offered to organise a day out for my son's arrival, the son from my previous marriage, I loved her a bit more but kept it to myself. I asked her to come, hoping she would, she told me she would have to see.

Her:
It was within my power to help ease his anxiousness, so I did. I had organised a day out

and he asked me to come along. I wanted to take him up on the offer but only to say goodbye and to allow myself to take the new job and be able to move away without dragging the pieces of my heart along with me. I knew I would go on to my new chapter with the knowledge that my future could now lay with someone, to know that I had the potential and capacity to love. To know that great relationships start from friendships. That knowledge itself was a gift, a gift that I could take away from all that pain.

Him:
She arrived for our day out together and when I saw her, I saw her deeply. I wondered how on earth I had been so stupid. As the day progressed my son had warmed to her - she had that effect. We went swimming at the end of the day, I'm not sure if the black bikini that clung tight round her body, like my hands had longed to, was for my benefit but it worked. It was the final straw. As my animal instincts took over completely I kissed her. I knew as perfect as it was that I had already done the damage by not being stronger sooner.

Her:
A perfect day some might say, but I could not do it, I knew he was in a different place, he was where I had been in the winter, ready for something to start, but time had wedged a hole between us and we had found ourselves in different places. The wrong time and the wrong place, with the perfect person. That day was my goodbye, my 'leave it on

a good note'. Our friendship had once again changed, but as the saying goes - All good things must come to an end.

Him:
My time with my son had been made so much easier from that day out together. We didn't see her again, I could tell that was her intention. My son talked about her, asking me if she was my girlfriend, and when I asked him if he wanted her to be my girlfriend he had said she was nice and that she was nice to him. What I couldn't say was, "well your dad screwed it up, so sorry mate."

My son had gone with my mum, his grandma, for the afternoon and as I travelled through the villages in the truck with my brother to help him pick up logs, I asked him what he thought mum would think if I brought someone home for a weekend. I didn't know if she would accept but I had to ask her, I couldn't let it be goodbye. Anyway, it was not the kind of conversation that my brother and I would generally have. I could tell he found it insignificant, but I needed to talk to someone about it. I had only asked two other people to my mother's house, one I married and one I had a child with. I knew what this meant; I knew that I needed her forever, but would she accept now - was it all too late for such momentous gestures?

Her:
He called me up with his son on the loud speaker -

he used his son's desire to speak to me as an excuse, I'm sure. His son was sweet in temperament, a soft natured child, asking curiosities about where I was and what I was doing. In truth though, at this stage I was keen to protect my heart and stop answering his phone calls. I couldn't help but answer though, and it was this need that annoyed me.

Him:
I was due to take my son back to his home country, it was a day travelling into Europe to get him back to his home. When the time came to leave I had already given it considerable thought and I knew I had to call, I had to be sure I could follow it through this time, that guilt would not get the better of me. So I called her.

Her:
I wanted to stop picking up the phone, he was calling and I knew it must be nearly time to take his boy back. Maybe his son had wanted to say goodbye to me, so I thought it best to pick up but this, I decided, would be the last call I would take from him. So I was extremely surprised when he went on to ask me to come to his mum's for the weekend. He was different in some way, more definite, more insistent that this was what would happen. I had a choice of course, which he gave me, but I felt he was so sure of this invite that it was impossible to turn him down. I told him I would need to think about it. He told me he would call me when he arrived back from dropping his

son off, and that he would drive past my house so that we could drive there together. I hated being a foregone conclusion but I told him we would see. I didn't pack for the weekend, I settled down to watch a movie instead, convincing myself that I wouldn't go if he called, that he was unlikely to call anyway.

Him:
When I called her as I arrived back in the country I expected her to turn me down. I knew she was moving on, I knew I had lost the commitment from her I could have so easily had in the beginning, all those months ago. As the phone rang, I feared she had decided not to take me up on the offer. When she finally did pick up, my heart leapt. She would meet me at the petrol station and follow me down south.

Her:
After he called, I packed up a bag for the weekend and thought, this is it now just one last weekend. I arrived at the petrol station, my heart was no longer at risk, I had decided not to commit myself into a friendship with him or in any other way. So when he arrived at my window with snacks for me for my journey his words made me realise that once again we had found ourselves in different places at different times. He told me that he had only taken two other people to meet his mother, the woman he married and the woman he'd had a child with, and casually said "just so you know". He was obviously trying to tell me how important

this was and where he was emotionally. I just wasn't there, my heart had decided to leave the thrashing tides of love and sit on the sidelines to watch the motions happen in other people's worlds.

Him:
...and so it began, I lost myself in her. I managed to get her to visit more than one weekend, and then every weekend. Somehow I had magically managed to keep her with me. I was a child again with her in my life. I committed to her, I admitted my quirks and she accepted me with them all. My failures, she said, were lessons that you learn in life, it's only if you keep repeating them that you really fail. I could still sense I had hurt her, she was holding back but this time I was determined to prove that I would not hurt her again. I would put everything I had in me to show her. It became the summer of love, and as I entwined myself into her life I found that I could not last even a day without talking to her. I had to know what she was doing. I sent her love letters through email. We had walks on the moors and I wanted to put romance and enjoyment at the forefront of everything we did. I needed her to want me as much as I wanted her. When she was sick, I wanted to take care of her. She now lived on the other side of the country due to my fears and inability to commit, so travelling every weekend was the only way, but the distance was too much for me emotionally. I was close to leaving it all so I

could be with her all the time. She was more sensible and said that time would allow us to work something out. I was still not convinced that she wanted it that as much as I did.

I would write to her when I was not with her, send flowers, anything to remind her that I was in it for the long-term, that I would not repeat the mistakes of my past.

On 6th July 2011, at 19:00, He wrote:

Hello you,
I thought I'd surprise you by putting pen to paper (so to speak) and just drop you a line as part of my plan to make sure you don't forget about me. I have found myself today struggling with the concept that we seem to be destined for a relationship that consists of weekends of love and a week of painful singledom.
Don't panic, this ain't me telling you that I'm off to Afghanistan, far from it! This is me telling you how it pains me to be apart from you and there is a good reason for that (well reasons to be more exact):
1. You're so lovely
2. I'm besotted with you
I have been searching for jobs near you and think I may just have got myself a job as a cleaner in the pub you ate your tea in! lol
You're a gorgeous, caring, passionate, intelligent, sexy chick and whilst it may have taken us awhile to get sorted (my fault of course) we're in it now and long may it continue.
I love you soooo much, don't forget that and don't let me forget it either. Talk later you :) Love me
xxxxxxxxx

Her:
It was the summer of love and growth. I was still wary of heartbreak, not quite ready to fully submerge myself into the thrashing waves. I knew I loved him, I had loved him longer than even I would care to know or admit. However, this did

not mean I was where he was. He insisted on speaking to me every day, even when there was nothing to say. He told me I made him feel like he was 18 again and that he never expected it. It was a strange kind of comfort to know that he was likely to get more hurt than I, which seemed sadistic as I would never want him to be hurt, it just seemed a safer position to be in. I had not allowed him to meet my parents or come to my new home. I was not ready to bring down those barriers but I always responded to his messages of love.

On 6th Jul 2011, at 21:00, She wrote:

My love,
What a lovely email, I am not sure you have understood that I love you for the person that you are, it's not just because of the intimacy we share but everything about you.
You give me everything I need or want from a partner, which for someone like me who wants the best of both worlds is pretty impressive. :) At this stage of a relationship I would have already gone or found faults as to why we wouldn't have a future but I don't have any with you. If we always try to respect each other neither of us will forget how special the other is.
I am sure distance won't be a problem for too long babes, decide what you want and we can plan around that. :) xxx Best tell me things on your bucket list too. :)

Love, me. xxx

Him:
Once the back end of the summer had begun to roll in she asked me to meet her parents. I knew this was a huge barrier being dropped, and the following weekend I went to her home. She had told me last time that her home had not felt like a place she could stay after I broke her heart and for that she was wary to allow me back in. I was so happy, so pleased that she might realise how committed I was, that I could not imagine my life without her, that I could not function without her. It was getting worse, my need to know if the rest of my life would be with her.

By the end of the summer she had left her job and I was asking her to move in with me. I wanted to find our perfect home.

Her:
I didn't care where we lived, as long as we were together. I knew I loved him, I had told him enough but still my heart was reserved, I knew that. We had spent the back end of the summer in a whirlwind romance that involved celebrations and parties. But turbulence loomed as we tried to find each other.

Arguments and emails ensued as we tried to find a way through the uncertainty and the fear of committing to each other forever. The end was looming over us like the grim reaper, reminding us that if we could not find a way to make it work this whole affair would be over.

On 9th Oct 2011, at 21:58, He wrote:

You left despite me asking you to stay, but then you always seem to want to apportion the "blame" for our many break-ups on me, which is very strange considering your admitted history of breaking up. I admit that my reaction last night was well over the top but then so would you be if you saw it coming and could do nothing about it and then went into defensive mode to protect your own sanity, and even now it appears as if you really are not that bothered. I for one have been sooo sad today and don't know what I'm going to do without you in my life as I really thought this was it for me, how wrong could I have been, eh?
You are right to mention my doubts about you and they have simply been proven right, even agreeing that I am to blame for it all doesn't avoid the fact that at no point yesterday did you seek anything other than you walking away, as you always do. It doesn't matter what I do, the end result is the same..... you go. I now have doubts about everything that we were all about, because surely if you really thought so much about us then it wouldn't have been so easy to walk away, which it seems it was for you. As for the Nov trip, I have paid for things that are really only of use to you and to say that I'm sad we won't do them together is an understatement, but I guess you'll never know now. I am going to continue house hunting in the hope that this is just another phase and guess that even if we really are over I need to get my own place anyway.
I am so so so sad girl, 2 songs that are particularly

apt....one you know very well as its all about us and one Bruno Mars song that sums up how I feel for you:

I'd catch a grenade for ya
Throw my hand on the blade for ya
I'd jump in front of a train for ya
You know I'd do anything for ya
I would go through all this pain
Take a bullet straight through my brain
Yes I would die for you, baby

Settle down with me
Cover me up
Cuddle me in
Lie down with me
And hold me in your arms
And your heart's against my chest, your lips pressed in my neck
I'm falling for your eyes, but they don't know me yet
And with a feeling I'll forget, I'm in love now.
Kiss me like you wanna be loved
You wanna be loved
You wanna be loved
This feels like falling in love
Falling in love
We're falling in love
Settle down with me
And I'll be your safety
You'll be my lady
I was made to keep your body warm
But I'm cold as the wind blows so hold me in your arms   Oh no! My heart's against your chest, your

lips pressed in my neck
I'm falling for your eyes, but they don't know me yet
And with this feeling I'll forget, I'm in love now
Kiss me like you wanna be loved
You wanna be loved
You wanna be loved
This feels like falling in love
Falling in love
We're falling in love
Yeah I've been feeling everything from hate to love to lust
From lust to truth I guess that's how I know you
So I hold you close to help you give it up
So kiss me like you wanna be loved
You wanna be loved
You wanna be loved
This feels like falling in love
Falling in love
We're falling in love
Kiss me like you wanna be loved
You wanna be loved
You wanna be loved
This feels like falling in love
Falling in love
We're falling in love

I loved you soooo much, unreservedly, I still love you , madly, and always will.

I had to write to her again, I sat fearing the end, having no control over her, her feelings, the future I had planned, it was all out of my control. All I had was the wonders of the written word to try to convince her.

On 10th Oct 2011, at 10:44, He wrote:

I wouldn't feel like I'd tried enough if I didn't have one final attempt to salvage something from the ashes. I realise a lot has been said by both of us and that things have gone so far but I must try and I want to try. Like I tried to explain last night, I admit that I over reacted on Saturday but I guess that's due to a combination of the poor timing, the knowledge that this was the start of a downward spiral leading to a massive argument (confirmed in a self fulfilling prophecy!) and the fact that I can't seem to stop you doubting us. Our relationship has been one fantastic adventure and at times it has reached heights that some/most will never ever attain and I honestly felt it would never end and I don't know what I'm going to do without you. We had felt like a large magnet was pulling us together, so I struggle to understand how, when we argue, it destroys all that - and it doesn't help of course that I am still madly in love with you.

Is it that you can easily walk away, you can be honest as I'd rather that then never knowing? I don't get it as I'm sitting here hurting like mad and feel physically sick at the thought that we really are finished. If you're feeling the same (and I hope you are?!) then that's a sign that there's something there, though I guess conversely if you're not going through the same then you should just tell me that I've got this wrong. Cards on the table from me......I love you, so much you will never know, far too much. I really did think that we were going to be together forever, it was that good being with you. You light up a room when you walk in and we both fit so well together, it can't be wrong. Ever since we got back together I have tried so hard to make you feel safe with me, as your partner and let you know that I was going nowhere and I've clearly failed miserably. Ed Sheeran and Bruno Mars can only have been writing about us when they wrote their songs as they fit 100%. I'm not playing any games and if you really feel there is nothing left to say or do and you want this to be the end then please just say but until I hear you say it I'm going to remain clinging on to the hope that our love just suffered a temporary knock and that with a deep and heartfelt discussion, it will return to normal service. Am I so wrong to believe that we were made for each other?

I'm hoping of course that this email will pull us back from the brink and doesn't come too late but if it doesn't and you believe it to be too late then just tell me and I'll try and leave you alone, though it's not going to be easy considering what you mean to me and where I believed we were going and if that is the case I don't know how I'm going to manage. I would try some big gesture to attempt to save us but I remember you saying how you feel that as embarrassing and that people should just get on with it, but believe me when I say I'm struggling not to. It seems to me as if you just don't understand how good you are and the effect you have on people and until you do you won't be able to understand why I love you so much as then you wouldn't doubt me anymore.

Guess I'd better bring this email to an end which is actually very hard to do as whilst I'm still writing it

I still believe us to still be a couple but once sent that may no longer be the case dependent on your reply...If I even get a reply. So that's it, my last clinging to life email is finished and ready for sending. Has it worked.....I so hope so. What if it hasn't and too much has happened for you.....I'll be devastated that I let you slip out of my grasp when I had you. What if there is a faint glimmer of hope....I'll do ANYTHING and EVERYTHING to save us and make you confident in us and believe in me/us.....anything. If I was with you now I'd get down on my knees and beg you not to bring us to an end and I'd be crying as much as I'm crying now....its bloody hard seeing a screen with tears in your eyes!

I love you so so much, you're my best friend and my sounding board for advice and the person I think about all day of each and every day, have I blown it with my stupidity and anger....maybe. If that is the case will I regret it for the rest of my life.....definitely. So all that's left for me to say is please can you find it in your heart to forgive me for my stupidness which was caused by being out of my depth and fearing exactly what happened in the end, like a self fulfilling prophecy. I'd do anything for you, please give me the chance to show you. Bruno and Ed know you know! lol

Love you truly, madly, deeply.

Over to you now babes, my heart is in your hands....please hand it carefully back if you no longer want it but I'd love you to keep it. Hoping for the best but terribly fearing the worst.

All my love always regardless of the outcome.

Love me :) xxx

Her:
I forgave him of course. I think maybe I always would as long as I knew we would move forwards, and for that I was able to open up a little more each day, because if the relationship grew a little more each day, I could always forgive.

Him:
I feel so proud to be with her all the time and I have now found our dream place. I had wanted to find it, it gave me a chance to show her how much I want this, how much I need her. I cannot be without her. She had wanted to live by the sea all of her life and I wanted to live in a cottage and that is what I found. A cottage by the sea. She's so excited, I wanted her to feel this to move in with me not just about living by the sea. I just want to make her happy, I want to make her happy forever. I fear I may not, I won't be able to change but I personally always feel I need to change to make anyone truly happy.

Her:
He has done the house hunting. I didn't want to, I needed to know he really wanted to move in with me and this was how he could show me. I know I want to, I just wasn't going to say it out loud, just in my head, to myself, lots and lots. If he finds it, if he is willing to make the effort then he obviously wants it. He sent me pictures of the beach, a tree that looked like it had seen more storms than the average tree and already I loved it. I rushed there between meetings and ran around in my high

heels. I called him, asked him if it was what he wanted, he had said yes, and I said well it's what I want too. I could have been in a cardboard box if it had been with him, but I never said as much.

Him:
I go to Ikea and love it. I know, hard to believe, but I feel so comfortable with her in my company. This has already been said hasn't it! I can be myself, truly myself around her. I didn't realise how much I haven't been myself in my life, I have been hiding in the shadows. I realised I did not need to change at all, that I am just happy being my true self, and she made me because she loves me for who I am.

Her:
I always thought I'd be terrible living with someone. I have never been able to live with a house mate, actually I have been terrible at it, always preferring my own mess and space, but when you are so entwined with someone it's different. It feels different, you are intrinsically linked and move around each other in a synchronised formation that feels like it is comfortably choreographed.

Him:
Oh God, it's so much better than I thought. Last time I did this it was a nightmare. I was secretly dreading it, thinking that there could be a re-run of the arguments and mess and complete opposites that emerged from the last time I moved in with

someone. But with her it's different, weird, like we were always meant to be here, in this house, together.

Her:
So of course we argue, we argue in a passionate way, in an 'I love you too much' way, an 'I don't know how to tell you the immenseness of my feelings for you' way. You are perfect for me, so perfect that it bubbles up and I find it so often has nowhere to go. So yes, we have arguments that end up in kisses. That's the way it works, our arguments, they happen on occasion and that's how they end. In a tangle of love, so intense that neither of us know where it will end. Then it happened, he was hugging me, getting me out of the dark place I was in. I could feel myself melting into him, that is the only way I can describe it, it felt in my mind that we were becoming one being, I no longer felt like a lone person, I felt greater than before.

Him:
So I've planned a weekend away for us. I just want it to go so well; I hope she will love it. She'd mentioned when we were first together a band she'd wanted to see - I wasn't that keen but I was sure I could do one night of them. I have found that love has made me forget the boundaries of my own contentment, so that I can now focus on what makes her happy. What can I do to make her life a little easier, a little lighter of the stresses and strains that life presents us. I have so often to hold

myself back from constantly holding her in my arms. If I allow myself even a moment's thought of not being able to make her happy I can feel my tears well up. Maybe this is how actors do it on the TV, maybe they are all in love as much as I am.

Her:
He took me away for a weekend, kept it all a secret until we arrived at whatever activity we were due to complete. I eventually discovered we were going to watch football in Germany with his German friends. I fell in love with him so much more then, watching him laugh so wholeheartedly, speaking another language so fluently. Every moment felt as though I knew him a little more. Then when I thought that was it, he surprised me by going to see one of my favourite artists ever: Bon Iver! I was ecstatic! It was a tiny venue, and just amazing. I could see all of the effort he had put into every detail as we wandered around the German market, so comfortable in each other's company it was hard to remember what it was like to be alone in the world.

Him:
So it is my Christmas work do with my regional clients tonight. Quite a few people are here, all with partners. I am waiting for her to arrive, I feel my heart swell with pride at the thought of having her by my side, and we have booked a room to stay the night. I am so excited to see her. She has been so busy at work recently that she always ends up

being late for everything - but that's ok, most of the time anyway. I've called her to ask her where she is, she has said she can't make it. I sank with disappointment. I can barely contain myself and wondered if she even felt what I felt. I don't want to be here at the hotel.

Her:
After a wonderful weekend I could feel his anxiety, so I shouldn't have joked that I wasn't going to make it to his work do due to my own work commitments. We'd had a great time in Germany, but I could feel something brewing and I just wasn't sure how this was going to play out. We had the usual hysterical laughter, this time over me going to the wrong room and standing seductively in the doorway. Whoops! We did all the niceties to his colleagues, I smiled with the people that cause him hassle at work and was smiling sweetly even though I feel particularly protective of him, though he certainly does not need it when it comes to work. When we got home the next day the weekend was upon us, our favourite time. He sat me down like he had been wanting to say this particular thing for his entire life: he said he doesn't feel as though I am in this as much as he is. He didn't want me to react, he just wanted to tell me that that was how he felt.

Of course, I was shocked but in truth maybe not surprised. I have been holding back. I was cautious to leave the hurt parts of my heart firmly where they were. I am not ready to give him those last tiny vulnerable bits, I don't want them to get hurt again. I told him I love him, but words weren't going to cut it. He went on to tell me it doesn't matter to him, he will never want to leave me, even if he loves me more than I can ever love him, that he will live with that because he wanted to be with me so much, more than he could ever remember feeling. 'As long as I never left him', he said. That was the biggest shock; he is so in love with me that he wants to be with me regardless, he wants to spend his whole life making me happy. He is already so happy, he feels like he just needs to make me happy too.

I have always, from the very beginning, made my terms clear: that should I ever fail to make him happy he must leave. I would not hold him back. He said he couldn't live without me, but if he wasn't going to be able to make me happy he would let me walk away - but he wanted to be given the chance, that was what he said.
No response of words was going to match this, to swell the emotion that he had generated, no grand declaration from me would cut it. I couldn't now tell him how long I had truly loved him, that my life is him, that I can feel his feelings, that all the things he feels ashamed for, all the things he dislikes about himself are the very things I love. A love that comes without expectation, need or wanting, just love that accepts.

So as I sat there listening as he poured out his inner feelings, his hopes and insecurities, I had nothing to say. So I simply said, 'I'm sorry'.

Him:
I decided on the spur of the moment that I would just tell her, tell her about how I feel. She had never judged me, she believes in honesty, so what was the worst that could happen? I couldn't continue to feel such uncertainty, that I was not making her happy, it would drive me crazy. All she could manage was 'sorry'. We hugged and kissed for the rest of the day, lost in each other. I feel better about it, and I just hope this moment never ends.

Her:
So I make an effort with everything now. In truth, I have been lazy because he always makes all the effort with little surprises, unexpected treats and generally spoiling me rotten. He still runs the baths and puts the tea on for us. But I have made sure that I make time to adore him, to focus and concentrate on giving up those last little pieces of my heart I have been holding on to, giving them up to him. The change is so subtle that no one but him would even notice.

January has come and I have been making a conscious effort to make plans with him, to enjoy walks on the beach, to finish work at a reasonable hour. Humour and banter has always been part of our friendship and now our relationship, but as I give up the remaining parts of my heart it plagues us like neither of us could have imagined. I have been learning that to truly experience life, you have to give all of your heart, to face the fear of rejection and just do it anyway.

We'd always spent our weekends together but now it feels as though things have evolved. The more time we spend with my family, and particularly my grandfather who I was always reluctant to share with any of my boyfriends, the more comfortable it all feels. He fits in perfectly. We made outdoor fires with my grandfather, the two of them competing on whose would be the biggest; the similarities between them, my two favourite men, makes me smile with happiness. I feel truly blessed.

Christmas came around and I had bought a weekend in Amsterdam - the only thing I could afford from our bucket list. We'd talked about a holiday together in the summer, somewhere in the sun, just the two of us. For now, I thought, this would do.

Him:
So she sat me down in January and asked me if I felt that she was in it as much as I was now, whether I felt the love from her as much as she did from me. I had to say yes now, I really did, I knew she was giving herself to me, all the broken pieces that we were putting back together. She let me take care of her, rely on me. When she told me that she genuinely saw no other life with anyone else and that she always believed that I was the first person she truly wanted to marry and be with until the end of time, my heart leapt and I felt a euphoria like I'd never known before.

Her:
I didn't quite expect the reaction that I got. I told him, 'I love you, I don't see my life with anyone but you'. He jumped on me, hugging me like I had given him a winning lottery ticket - if I'm honest, it felt something of an overreaction; it just didn't feel relative to the news I'd given to him. I thought this was old news, I thought it was quite trivial. Then I realised how closed off I'd been. Of course I don't think I've made him unhappy, not by any means, but he has had this fear that I would leave him and that all my broken pieces might never heal, and now that I have given him those pieces - all of them, unreservedly - he feels as though I'm finally his.

Him:
I am done, she is my life. There is nothing more I need - no material items, just her and my

children's health. She has taught me to forgive myself, to allow my spirit to be free. I can be myself now, my whole self. January has passed us by and as February approaches I have made a real effort for her for valentine's day. The valentine's I had missed last year still weighed on my mind. I never wanted to miss another chance to show her how much she means to me.

I have taken a ring of hers for sizing purposes. I told her that I was doing it, but I waited until after valentine's had passed. I didn't want to get it wrong and for her to be disappointed. I planned to do it on a summer holiday, when we had some money for the ring; she won't care what the ring looks like, I know that, I just want it to be right. There is no pressure, just love and honesty that allows a freedom and peace between us that feels safe.

Her:
March was a time of planning, and we had already decided on all the places we wanted to go. We were now looking at possible business opportunities, things we could do outside of work. He did not want to do the job he was doing for the rest of his life and I want to support him. We want to do something together, so that's what we plan to do. I feel even more connected to him now, like suddenly we are free to plan a life together. We had already told each other, as friends, that marriage and children were not something we ever wanted to enter into; something that, while I

stuck with it, he quickly dissolved when asking for my ring size.

Him:
I never dreamt I could dream as much as I do with her. That I have an idea and she helps me make it a reality. Everything in my life with her has made opportunity a possibility. After we had attended a franchise show in London, I'd returned overwhelmed by her support. We climbed into bed that night and as I cuddled into her I could feel the tears falling, they wouldn't stop. She turned to ask what was wrong, but I couldn't describe it any other way than to say that whilst I had so much happiness in my life, my first wife - who I had let down so momentously - was not happy. I felt I didn't deserve the happiness I now felt with her. She has taught me to release the guilt but that doesn't mean the sadness is not going to leak out too. She held me and let me cry; she had seen me cry more than any other person. It was like releasing a lifetime of having to 'be strong'. That's life though isn't it, I have learnt. Be strong, don't cry, don't let someone see your weakness, never admit your mistakes. As I lay with this beautiful woman who loves me for me, I could quash all those myths and feel greater than I had ever felt. I feel free, and true freedom comes only when you let go of the ego, the material needs, the past and the regrets.

Her:
I feel so excited about what is to come. Spring is

now here, we have made a list and we are looking at ideas for what business we might set up together, something that could grow and he would enjoy. I'm going to help, of course, but I just want him to be happy and feel free. It feels like we have become even stronger and intrinsically linked, that I know what he is thinking before he thinks it. I have come to realise that though I thought I knew what love was, I really didn't. I knew a type of love. This is more than that, this is making someone greater by your existence, accepting someone for who they are and they you, with all your crazy faults, that they love you just the same. We laugh so much and are so synchronised in our approach to life. I knew he would ask me soon, I just couldn't wait now!

Him:
The worries creep back every so often but I know I can speak to her, I know she will always make it better. It all feels so perfect, it feels like something might come and ruin it at any time. Maybe the jealousy of an external person coming into our little bubble? Maybe something else? As we lay in each other's arms chatting about the day, I shared my fear. Of course, she never dismisses it out of hand, she allows me to talk, to get it out.

Her:
He is perfect. We are in mid-March and the weather is warming up. A bath was the last thing I wanted but after tea and to have some time alone to talk about our days and our future it was just

what I needed. As I rested back he kissed my forehead and held me like he would lose me. He told me everything was so perfect for him, he thought something was going to come along and ruin it for us. I reassured him of the things that were improving, where we were. I told him, he must speak to his ex wife, tell her how sorry he is; he had never apologised for cheating on her and he felt that maybe she just wouldn't care to hear it now. I told him she may not, but also she may, so he had to. We talked until he felt assured of the fact that we are in control of our own destiny, that nothing could come along and ruin it if we chose not to allow it in. We are in control of our future together, as a team, and we would be even greater tomorrow than today.

Him:
As I watch her shower after the bath, which I always found a strange concept. She admits some misdemeanours of her past, things she could carry guilt for, but she has chosen not to because she has learnt to forgive herself and has made her apologies if not in person then to the universe. It all seemed a bit silly to me but she seemed so free of burden that I thought I might try it too. As I watched her, I never thought I would be attracted to someone like her, but I am; she's my Cheryl Cole, that's what I would call her, slim and petite. I can't imagine being with anyone else now.

Her:
I love how much we rely on each other and as I

rush home early from work, because the sun is shining, I drag him onto the beach with a drink to watch the sunset. I can feel the warmth on my face, he will leave tomorrow to head up to Scotland for the day and I already miss him. His mind seemed a little lost today but I never have any fears over his love for me, he will tell me what it was in due time, I have no doubt about that.

Texts 22ⁿᵈ March 2012

Him: Love you babes :) xxx

Her: Love you too babes. :) xxx soooooo much

Him: Well that's fine but I'll always love you more! Lol

Him: Where are you Luce? :'(

Him: Give me a bell babes not heard from you :) xxx

Him: Forgot to bring my photo ID licence, thank god for my old army ID card in my wallet in the car!! Lol

Her: Jeez. and you call me an admin nightmare. Safe travelling baby. :) xxx

Him: No idea what I've done with it as it's normally with my other cards!

Him: Anyway, boarding now so turning phone off. Laters you :) xxx

Her: Lol. Ummm looks like your licence has decided that my purse is a nicer place to be! Lol. They are both together.

Him: What better place for me to be than right next to you! Just landed in a very sunny Glasgae :) xxx

Him:

When I arrived back from Scotland I knew I had to call my son. My ex answered, and because he was not immediately available for the first time in four years we had a brief chat. I asked her how she was. I felt that I was softer, less protective of myself, I knew myself now and being hard on the phone through my own guilt was not serving either of us very well. We chatted for a few minutes, but I never said sorry, maybe next time, next time it would be easier now that we have started to talk again.

Her:

He was lost in his thoughts when he returned, telling me how he'd had a conversation with his ex-wife but not managed the sorry that he still didn't quite feel was timed correctly. He had loved her at some point and he didn't want her to feel bad, but he also didn't want to dig up old wounds. I told him he would get a chance, his chance to air it would come.

I often thought that if it was easier, if things did not seem so troublesome, I would have maybe walked away after one of those early arguments. But in an alternate universe where it may have been brighter, to me it wouldn't have been, it would be different and different would have been so much duller.

Chapter Two

The big day.

Her:

When the day arrives that will change your life forever, you may at first feel surprise. You may feel shock or grief; if you're lucky you may even feel joy. But whichever emotion should manifest itself in the moment, once you step back to take a deep look inside of yourself you soon come to realise that that day was, and always had been, just around the corner.

We'd arranged our schedules so as to have the whole week off together, and so we were looking forward to some quality down time, both the two of us alone and with his son, whom we'd arrange to pick up later in the week. He'd also agreed to take part in a charity cycle ride. When I had said I wouldn't be there to support him on the second day he had been disappointed, and had encouraged me to go along to watch, which I reluctantly agreed to. It is so nice knowing that we have some time off together, but really I just wanted to get all of my unfinished work stuff out of the way - as I know he has surprises in store for the rest of the week.

I have dropped him off at the starting point and he seems quiet, not putting his hand on my leg as he usually does, and oddly distant as though his thoughts are consumed by something else. I wondered what it was. I wondered what was about to enter my life.

Of course, he becomes the joker once he finds the

others so I hope it was not something he was hiding from me. As I drive away, I'm compelled to pull-over and message him, to tell him that I love him, that if he wants me to move my meetings to come and get him, or to stay to support him, then I could do that. He didn't respond, but I knew I had told him and that he knew I had offered.

I hope he's not falling out of love with me, that his heart is still mine.

Her:
Good luck today babes. Just call me if you need me to come and get you but you'll be fine. Xxx

I got to work and then he called to tell me.

Him:
I wasn't quite sure I had made the right choice in joining the cycle ride - it did look good for work, though. I don't do enough things like this. In my new life with her I have become much more of a 'yes' person; it suits me, I like it. Besides, it's too late to back out now. I had asked her if I should do it, she had her usual stock response, 'you should do what makes you happy, if you don't want to, don't, but if you feel you will be disappointed by not doing it then you should do it'. I wanted her to tell me not to and that the idea of 180 miles was preposterous. God, I love her so much. Marriage, life, I cannot imagine a day in my life without her and I am excited about asking her even though I know what her answer will be.

Him: *Now at Bath and dying! Absolutely buggered!!*

Her: *Lol. Keep going babes your legs are made of steel. :) xxx*

Him:

I can't see the messages, so I call her - my vision is blurry. I tell her I don't feel well, that I need to call an ambulance. She wants to know where I am. I don't want her to worry, I have to call her back, and then it goes black.

Chapter Three

The ramblings of immediate loss.

It's a strange moment when your life slows down. I was barely able to believe what was happening, thinking: 'This doesn't really happen.', 'It's all just a very surreal dream.' 'If I can just shake myself out of it.'

That's what happens, you see. It's just a normal day, you are just talking, laughing, planning about nothing much and then everything changes in a lost heart beat.

23rd March 2012

As I sit in the hospital I can barely believe I am in this situation, where the man I saw trying to save your life comes to tell me that there is nothing more they can do, that 'I am sorry but his life has expired.....'.

I think he carried on talking to me after that, but I can't be sure. I cannot speak any words and thoughts are lost, I sink to the floor as the chair seems to be moving. I cannot see, visually or metaphorically. The world I know no longer exists, and that realisation seems impossible. I feel like someone is playing a weird trick on me, like it was a test of my love for you. Maybe it is. Maybe this is an elaborate hoax because you want to get out of your love with me. But you can't have died, it seems too impossible, too unreal to believe that's what happened. I'm rambling... words and thoughts make no sense.

I need the toilet constantly which is strange as I haven't drunk anything - or have I? - I don't know. They've put me in a room, laid me down on the sofa with a blanket and I stare at the 1970s curtains that the sun dared to peek through.

All I feel is filled with love, your love.

So when a nurse sits down to ask how I am, I keep staring at those curtains. But I tell her everything about you, about us, how perfect you are, how lucky I have been to have known you. I don't know how long I was talking, but when I eventually turned to her she had silent tears of someone who wished she hadn't heard it, wished she hadn't seen your dead body, the one she and her colleagues had tried to save even when you had long gone. They never wanted to give up even when they didn't know you or us. So in that moment when I turned to her, I felt bad for upsetting her, for telling her what I had lost and all I could say was, 'I'm sorry'.

The day disappears in a fog of nurses, people holding my hand, your family's shock. When my parents arrive the tears come and the shock eases. My father tells me you are the only one that he actually liked out of all my previous poor decisions on partners, and I know you would have loved that.

People from work arrive at the hospital. They tell me that you're being given a tribute, that it's being given at the handing over of the cheque for Sports Relief in London tonight. I know you'd have loved that too. I can't work out time, I'm sure you've only been gone an hour, how could that have been organised in that time? I don't have the strength of mind to question it so I just give my appreciation on your behalf.

As I return in the evening to our dream home, the cottage by the sea that you found for us, I can barely contain myself. Your slippers are where you left them this morning, the photos of us, your beautiful children catch my eye. Your shelf in the study with all of your things. The 'I love you' messages that sit all over the house from you to me. They're on the boiler, every mirror, every window a heart has been placed, even on the inside of the freezer. How will I go on without you making me my cup of tea in my travel cup every morning and getting it from the car because I have forgotten it again? You never complained. You filled me with compliments and told me how happy you were, I feel there must be a way I can take it all back.

I sleep restlessly in a bed that smells of you and I don't know what I will do now without you here. You fixed the broken bits of me, and now I am more broken than I have ever been. Everyone keeps saying remember the good times, but I can't remember any bad, I was so lucky to have you in my life even though it was short.

The odd friend arrives to support me at our house today. I cannot contain my sadness darling, how will I ever go on without you? We had so many plans together.

24th March 2012

Darling, I have been in and out of sleep. I cannot bear to move anything in the house. You were perfect, I don't know what I will do without you, I cannot cope, please tell me what I should do to take this complete heartbreak away. How will I ever cope without you and our routines?

I have written on Facebook to tell people, the feedback has been unbelievable - and there was you always saying that you didn't have any friends. You were so loved. If I were to take something away from this, it's that we must tell each other in life what we all mean to each other. Let us not stand alone in life, as we didn't in our time together. I have always had friend and family support in my life, but your loss has made me feel so alone, even in this sea of support. I've made it to the afternoon, and as I cry, hopelessly thinking that someone will take pity on me and give you back, I smell your t-shirt to calm me down. What will I do when the smell goes, how will you help me?

You used to measure your popularity by how many people remarked on your status. Well in your death they are coming into the 50s, so I hope you are looking down.
The sun is shining so strongly, the summer that we had planned together still seems possible, I still think you will come back to me. I took a walk along the beach and thought about how we had

only been sitting there in the sun a few days ago, talking about the lovely time we would have, and the grief has overpowered me once again. I cannot see any future without you in it.

I feel I am looking for you in the dark, but I am unable to find you. Please help me.

The waves of grief consume me - how must everyone else feel? I don't know what I will do without you.

Spoke to my mum, she feels overwhelmed by the unfairness of it all. Everyone saw how wonderful we were together.

A few people came to the house, I made sure I showed them around, they were jealous of the walk-in wardrobe that you built for me, as you would have wanted them to be, of course. I wonder why today is the day they decided to visit. Why wait until today? Why wait until it's too late? The grief is united in these moments as we walk around the house and I tell them the stories of our life here together. I am aware I am a little crazed, so all over the place that I don't know myself but I don't know any other way at the moment. I repeat myself like I need mental help, I rant on repeatedly about how, 'we wont do this again'. It's all I have right now.

We sit and talk; all we are doing is drinking tea, you would love it. Your place at the end of table sits empty and there are times when I cannot contain my sadness; you and I know what we had but I feel like I cannot explain it to anyone else because it is only you who knows and you've gone. I realise no one came to visit us here, no one knew our life, this reality makes me so incredibly sad. Sometimes when I feel too alone I sit in your place to feel close to you again.

I come to bed, with your shirt and our brown blanket that you would wrap me up in with cuddles on the sofa. Yes, we just fitted my darling, no one will be made the same shape as you so even after this short time I am realising that I will be just one half of the puzzle for the rest of my life. Someone wrote something lovely on my Facebook wall, about a discussion you had had with her on your history of disastrous relationships but that you admitted you had finally felt you had met your soulmate... I find some comfort once again.

When I walked into the bedroom there was a big spider on the wall, it suddenly dawned on me that I would have to deal with it myself, a simple task, but one you had adopted for me. I can feel you with me, but without your body to convince me of your presence I feel lost. It is night number two without you, so I will imagine our usual nightly conversation, 'Night babes love you'... 'love you too'.

25th March 2012

I wake to the uncontrollable tears and not even your smell can help me this morning. I can't help it as I am still unsure where you are. I've composed myself and managed to get downstairs, I just keep in my mind what a wonderful man you were. I know you would want me to speak at your funeral and talk about our love and all that you did, as you always said you wanted the world to know. People seem unconvinced that I could do it and that I may need help to get through it.

I went through your phone, funny how you always said I could look at anything on your computer or phone and you had no passwords or had given them to me and then in your death is when I have to go through them. Nothing resonates more with me than that call you made before you died and the messages we had sent to each other with our declarations of love. When you got to Bath you messaged me saying you were knackered, should I have told you to stop? Would it have made a difference? Were you alone? Did you know I was there with you when they were trying to resuscitate you? Were you watching over me? I will never know your answers, so I try to remove them from my mind.

I don't know if I should go for the interview tomorrow. You didn't like my current job, I know... I think you'd tell me to be strong and do it.

I spoke to your ex-wife. You were right, she is a lovely lady. I told her how sorry you were. I wish you could have told her in person, maybe it was part of the bigger plan that I would tell her and I could help her through the journey. I am so happy that she has your son. She has a reminder every day of the young love that you had together. I wish you had stayed with me a little bit longer, I just needed a bit more time. But then sixty years would never have been enough for me. You said when you met me you had met your soulmate for the rest of your life, and it really was the rest of your life, just so much shorter than either of us could have imagined.

I've been to the church today to meet with the vicar - how can this be real, how can I place you in the ground? Baby, please come back and keep me warm, be my guide, laugh with me, I cannot bare the heartache. When my heart aches I feel it is yours, that I mirror your pain that day. You cannot leave me like this with no rhyme or reason. I need to know why you left me alone in so much pain.

I am remembering everything that we said to each other.

Sat in the bath, you said that this was so good that something would have to be good forever. Perfect, not perfect but I was perfect for you. I used to say I love you and you would say you can't love me because I have taken all the love in loving you. You said if something was ever to happen to me that you would give up as you could never find someone who fitted so perfectly with you. I said the same but I never thought only two weeks later I would find it to be true.

I'm sitting by the pond and can hear you telling me I need to go to the interview. You hated me in that job, I need you to support me though and get me through it. I have written the order of service. Please ensure that I am doing everything that you wanted; I am following my heart as that is where I feel you are.

26th March 2012

No tears. I went to bed with the blanket and your shirt. I woke up in the morning and knew you weren't going to be there, as much as I longed for it to be untrue. You always set the alarm clock 15 minutes earlier so we could have a cuddle before we got up, you always said that it was about the cuddles and you showing me how much you loved me. The morning that you died was the first time we just got straight up, I feel so sad for that. The stars were beautiful last night, I am so sorry I couldn't get that application working on my phone.

I still can't shower, I will wash you from me. I can't even take my clothes off or change, you were never very far away trying to get a cheeky glimpse. If I get changed, have a shower, go to the shops it means that everything starts to go on without you and I can't stand that.

The waves of sadness seem to be rising and I feel I am in danger of drowning. How can my heart physically ache, how does that happen? I don't have feelings in my heart only my head, is my heartache you telling me how you passed away? You leave me wondering if you are standing next to me, but in reality I know you have gone.

I am in the house, I am so used to seeing you in my eye, you looking over your laptop staring at me waiting for me to look up so you can give me a wink - the love I could see in your eyes. I cannot see you, what would I do to see you again?

The boiler stopped working again. It has failed the last three times when you have gone away and I wonder if it will pack up altogether now.

The sun has shone so brightly every day since you died, you would have loved it. How will I survive? The house is so quiet without you and Sky News is playing in the background.

27th March 2012

The sun is still shining and a card has come through the letterbox. I am not sure what I will do when the sympathy stops because then you are gone and there is just me. I am writing bits of your speech today. People keep telling me I will never forget, but I have to. I have to forget what we had because it was so perfect that if I don't forget I will no longer have a purpose to live.

I will get through your funeral and then I will need to forget. I wonder if I can get hypnotised to forget.

The boiler's fixed; it was the thermostat. The neighbours came round and cut the grass.

I see everyone just starting to write normal stuff on Facebook. How can they just carry on, how does life continue without you?

My birthday soon and I cannot think of anything less I would want to do.

Planning the funeral has commenced. The sun was setting on the beach and I can barely go there without a pain in my heart as I miss you and cannot imagine that you won't see it again. Night baby love you.

28th March 2012

The postman is coming again, and although I know it will be another card reminding me of your loss, I pray that you have sent me a birthday card so that I can have something from you telling me you are still here with me. I know my wishes will not to be granted. Today's card was from my aunt and uncle, the ones you were trying to remember the names of, and the cousins. It had a poppy on the front and made me cry when I read it as they described your loss as a cruel blow just when happiness had been found. They keep letting me know that I am in their thoughts. I know people are just carrying on with the day-to-day, how can they? How can they not realise what we are going through with your loss? Such a hole, a void that I will never fill. I feel more alone than I can even put into words.

I wrote to a girl from my past after finding her on Facebook, someone that I knew had lost her fiancée very early. I think it was you who told me to do it as it just popped into my mind. She gave me a comfort that no one else has been able to do. No one else can understand the loss of a partner so perfect, with our perfect life and perfect plans together. The same as I cannot understand the loss of a child. Our grief is our own, and that knowledge makes me feel alone again.

Your work bought flowers, I wish they had sent you back to me.

The funeral arrangements continue - most of it's sorted but if you could help out with the songs I would appreciate it.

29th March 2012

My friend arrived last night after a long drive. Everyone seems to have an inner fear of losing their partner, even the thought is enough to upset them. I am living it with the loss of you.

The neighbours have been round and watered the plants as the sun is still shining here. I can't watch daily daytime TV, I can't bare to watch the world carrying on, don't they know that you have gone, don't they know the pain I feel?

I click your phone to see it light up and your calendar reminds me it's my birthday tomorrow. I cannot imagine any birthday where I won't be reminded of you. I want to just forget, I want it all to be gone, what has happened?

Trying to sort out the bills. I am left with it to sort but I always did it anyway because that was my job. I sit in your seat now at the table, typing this to you each day, planning. I can't sit anywhere else, I used to love the sofa but that is increasingly difficult because you're no longer there to hold me. It's been five days and it feels like a lifetime, how will I possibly go on with life?

Just found texts from my other phone, it was from the early days and you said you'd rather be dead than without me - I am still here baby, but you left me alone, without you. Please, please I beg you to stop this.

Did you know this was going to happen, because I am starting to wonder whether you ever loved me? Did you know all along and this was just a cruelness that you have done to me? I am sorry, I know that's not true but the cruelness just seems to have no rhyme or reason.

'I treasure every day that you're my girl', is what you said.

I'm phoning up to sort the bills again: water sorted, tax I have to call again after Easter.

They told us yesterday that it was a blood clot that couldn't pass due to a thickening of the arteries in your heart. I am trying to get your death certificate sorted today but in a cruel twist it looks like it won't be ready until my birthday.

I found your driving licence in my purse and I want to scream but I have nothing left to shout at the injustice of it all. After I thanked you for selling my car for me, you replied, 'no thank you for being with me, I treasure every day that you are my girl Lucy.'

I am angry about that message, you know which

one, what a truly nasty person she is, she really was an absolute cow and I am sorry that she made those years of your life such a misery. I can't believe I was so nice to her on the telephone after you died but at that time I was in shock and if I'd truly known how horrible she was I wouldn't have said sorry for you as I know you didn't want to say that much. The core of her is rotten and mean. She bleats on about the kids interests being at heart but she behaves the complete opposite.

30th March 2012

My birthday. It's 4pm already and I have been sitting in your seat all day, unable to move, grounded to your chair. My birthday seems like a sea of sadness. Someone from your work came round. I had to compose myself, no one wants to come round and see a blubbering mess, so I made a cuppa - he got the drama queen cup, we were sure it was you in the background laughing about it. It's been a week since you died and I cannot cope without you, they keep saying it gets easier but I am not convinced. So much has happened. I went to the pub with people, I felt sad that you weren't with me holding my hand as you would have been but it's a step forward, though it makes it no easier. As I drove down to the farm yesterday to sort the funeral I went past the Glastonbury tour and thought of you. I thought about you blowing on the conch shell when you went to the toilet.

The look in your eye always said that you were proud of me, and to be with me. To have finally found the one, it seems such a cruel blow that you should have been taken so early. But I have no regrets. I know I expressed how wonderful you were to me, as a person, every day, through a look, a laugh or words.

You would also run your finger down the radiator in the hall. I miss the sound, I miss every sound and I miss you mostly my darling.

We left each other in no doubt as to the way we felt about each other; no regrets baby, I love you, please let me meet people like you in my life so I can have the love and laughter forever more.
You were always right, you were a great guide to me and kept me calm. You would help anyone even when they weren't necessarily deserving of it.

Only last week you cooked me dinner and ran me a bath and said how long it had been since we had bathed by candlelight as you massaged my head after a stressful day at work. You said it was so good between us that something would have to happen for it to end, but I don't imagine you thought this. I can't get this.

I feel if I move too quickly then the knife in my heart will plunge deeper, the hurt grow more unbearable.

31st March 2012

This morning seemed the worst, I miss you so much. If I could give up everything and live in complete whiteness that would surround us then I would do it, but I do not know where you are. Please tell me where you are so I know where to meet you.

11th April 2012 - The funeral

It had been a long time coming, this day. I wanted it to pass. So many times I had wished it could be that day again, the day you died, not because I thought for one moment that I could have you back again but just so that it at least wouldn't feel so long since I was last in your presence.

I had written the words in your honour; the words had flowed so easily from my hand onto the paper. I felt you would come to listen, wherever you were. I wanted to look nice for you, I wore the white dress that you loved so much, but kept my black jacket on so as not to offend anyone.

My thin frame was noticed by others, it was another reason for people to weep for the grief that they saw seeping out of me, deep within my eyes, my entire being lost in grief. They knew something that I didn't: that life was changed forever.

Yesterday I read the speech to the vicar, as I wanted to be sure I could do this for you. When I finished I asked him: 'Do you think it's too long? I don't want people to be bored or think I went on too much about my upset'. He kindly reassured me, 'People will want to hear what you have to say.' I noticed a tear in his eye and thought again that no one is immune to the ending of life, those that see it everyday do not get a pardon from the heartache.

The sun shone that day. I parked the car at the village hall, walked down into the village. I didn't want to be with anyone, I was with your ex-wife but did not feel her presence and she did not feel mine I suspect. I said hello to people, but I just wanted to stand. I tried to make people feel ok with words that would not have helped them or me. I stood outside the church feeling like it was a show, a performance where there was an end and everything went back to normal, like we were just acting this stuff out in the scene of a movie; it would end, it was all just a show right?

As the hearse pulled up, the rain came down and people disappeared for shelter. The irony was not lost on me.

We stood in the doorway behind your coffin which was being carried into the church by six chosen friends from all different walks of your life. One of them, I could see his shoulders shaking, his head bent to hide his tears, crying uncontrollably - but he had a duty. I felt sad he could not just run away as I suspect he wanted to, run away and leave the hurt behind. As we followed the coffin into the church the physical warmth of a full church hit me, I couldn't look. I hadn't realised how many people had arrived. I couldn't allow myself to be aware of their staring, I couldn't be aware of the grief of those around me. I just walked in with my head down.

It went as I had hoped. It was not a service full of 'woe is me', it was of the man that you were, full of laughter at any given opportunity. You had a story for every occasion, 'Did I tell you.....' was how you would start conversations to me, and there were lovely stories that followed the same ilk, like you had put the words into the mouths of your friends. They were just your puppets for the day.

I read last. The vicar did not introduce me, he just looked at me when it was my time to stand, I knew it was my cue. The church was silent but I could feel the apprehension, the wondering what I could say, whether I would get through it or if there would be a terribly sad and embarrassing moment as someone peeled me off the altar floor.

I did not look up, I just read.......

"Ben had told me we would get married, actually he worded it, 'Luce, I am going to marry you one day'. The week before he died he asked me what my dream wedding would be, and my answer was that all I asked for was Ben, our family and friends. He said he'd have to borrow some of my friends as he wouldn't be able to fill his side of the church and yet today, as we stand united in our grief for his loss, we can barely fit everyone in.

He loved Facebook as a way to connect with people. He would read out his status updates to me and measure their success by how many people had liked or commented on them. When we wrote about his death the comments and messages came in their hundreds. He always underestimated the effect he had on people and will continue to do so.

The summary of the messages describe him as many things: respected, liked by everyone, the life and soul, a great guy, a good friend, unique, genuine, lovely, always making time for people but the ones that resound close to my heart were kind, funny, generous and friendship.

FUNNY

He'd make me laugh daily, he'd call me fatty in front of friends and I'd call him grumpy, which was our ironic, sarcastic humour.

I remember one day, he was telling me that he loved me with such warmth and feeling, but I just turned to him and said 'that's nice dear' and he laughed at the dryness of it - that was our routine.

He would bring me snacks and do things with the food, like hearts placed on cheese on toast. On the other hand he would also bring me food that he'd strategically placed into embarrassing symbols - I'll leave it to the imaginations of those who knew him well. That was our routine.

He took great delight in tickling me, he loved to hear me laugh in as many ways as possible and tell it back to me, the way I had laughed. That was our routine.

I was often late back from work and as I opened the door he would greet me in various poses. His favourite was to moon me. He never stopped finding ways to make me laugh and start our evenings with humour. That was our routine.

Every morning he would look out of our window across the beach and tell me if he could see Wales or not, 'Cant see Wales, babes', 'Unfortunately, can see Wales babes', he only asked me last week if I must get annoyed by it, but I told him that I loved it. That was our routine.

We have two wooden people in the kitchen window that the neighbours pass by each day. Periodically he would change them into random and embarrassing positions. I dread to think what the neighbours must have thought but it never failed to make us laugh. That was our routine.

He would text landlines for his own amusement,

ours and his mums - for those that don't know how it comes across you must try it, although some of his are not to be repeated. The one I can tell is when I picked up the phone to hear, 'I love you Luce, you gorgeous, intelligent, caring, lovely woman' in the voice of a robot. It brought me to laughter yet again. That was our routine.

On his final day on this earth, when I dropped him for his cycle ride, he had bought new padded shorts. He took great delight and amusement in front of those who were around in sticking his bottom out and making me pat the padding. That was our routine.

KINDNESS

His kindness towards everyone was a given but he expected nothing in return, and that is the sign of a truly beautiful soul. Every morning he would set the alarm clock a little earlier for hugs and a chat to plan the day. That was our routine.

He'd go to get my travel cup from the car that I would always forget to bring in the night before, make me a cuppa and breakfast before sending me on my way with a spring in my step, he never complained. That was our routine.

Ben found our dream cottage by the sea and when we walked along the beach we always said how lucky we were and I told him how clever he was to find this home. That was our routine.

He always knew how much I appreciated everything he did for me and for that he said I deserved it all, but that was just his kindness. That was our routine.

He would tell me he loved the way I was with his children as the kindness, love and hugs that we had between us, I also made sure I shared with his children. The children worshipped Ben because of everything that he was and believed in. That was our routine.

When I was poorly, he would fuss over me and always make me feel better. That was our routine.

He wrote declarations of his love for me and left them as messages around the house, cards and notes for me to find, told me how proud he was to be with me and other compliments that filled me with confidence. That was our routine.

I would call him perfect. He would say, 'I am not perfect but I am perfect for you and you are perfect for me.' That was our routine.

GENEROSITY

Generosity for me is not measured by how much money a person has to give, it is what they give with their time and Ben offered it for free to anyone who needed it.

The measure of our love was not based on material things but what we did for each other, and he absolutely spoilt me, with affection, taking care of me and complimenting me but as you can imagine he spoilt me with humour. That was our routine

Every night he would get into bed first to warm up my side, he'd move over to let me into the warm side and then suffer the cold as he said he deserved it. His final words to me every night were always, 'Love you babes', and I'd say 'love you too'. That was our routine.

FRIENDSHIP

Ben was a friend to many but underestimated the impact that his friendship had. You couldn't help but like Ben, he had a presence.

We had been friends for several years before getting together. We worked together and would talk most days about work, ideas and usually some cheeky humour was thrown in by him for good measure. I cannot recall a time that I asked him for help in these years and he wasn't there for me, including a time when he had said he would meet me to help me to do a Bio report on site. The only time he could do was 6am on this particular day. We agreed a plan and left it at that, until the night before when I called to remind him. He'd completely forgotten and was down at his mum's house in Devon but never told me any of this; without my knowing he set off at 3.30 in the morning to drive all the way from Devon so that he wouldn't let me down. But that was Ben. I would refer to him as my best work friend.

As this trust grew between us, he started to call me up with life questions and ask my opinion on an idea he'd had to put his life in a different direction, sometimes not even allowing me time to say hello. Ben would be straight into retelling his thoughts or asking a question and wanting to know my opinion. One of these times he asked me, 'if you went out on a date with a man, it was all going well (he then went on to tell me all about a scenario of a great evening for the next 5 minutes) but then finally the guy went on to tell you that he lived on a barge, what would you think of him, would it be a deal breaker?'. He made me laugh, but he was thinking life on a barge would be peaceful.

When he walked into a room you knew Ben was there. Even my friends, who he had only met a few times, had let him work his way into their hearts - as he did with everyone. My friends and family adored Ben for all that he was, which was just himself. He was gold standard, we loved to spend time with his family and mine. That was our routine.

When I needed guidance Ben was there, he

levelled me like no one else had been able to. He would always talk to me about his worries and me to him, and we built a trust that can only come with true friendship. That was our routine.

When I was troubled he would link our hands together and tell me to remember we were linked like this forever. That was our routine.

Ben was a beautiful, uncomplicated soul who I found easy to understand and who then made me fall in love with him. For every joke that he made he also had an 'I love you', a hug, a compliment and statement of how happy and lucky he was in his dream cottage by the sea. He would tell me often that I had allowed him to be himself and for that he latched onto me so tightly and had such a fear of losing me that I would need to give him constant reassurance. I know that we never dreamed some three weeks ago that we would be here. We never took each other for granted and he said he didn't deserve the happiness we had, but I say he did, he deserved every moment. He may have felt misguided in the past but the core of him and the essence of him was that he was perfect, wonderful, funny, kind and generous. Although I will laugh a little less in my life from now on, the time I had with him was worth everything to me as some people search their whole lives never to find what we had.

If Ben were here today to give his lessons, he would say, be kind to each other as life is short, live each day with no regrets, don't forget to praise and appreciate one another as we did, laugh at your own mistakes and never take it all too seriously because tomorrow may never come.

I love you Ben and may you be looked after well wherever you may rest. When the sun shines you shine upon us and when it rains it is your sadness in not being with us".

People laughed at the right moments and were silent when needed. I kept my head down throughout the reading and then in the pin drop silence of the church, took my seat.

I had not thought beyond telling the story that you had so badly wanted to tell, I had focused on it, getting through it, doing it for you, it was so important. So when we filtered out, following the coffin to be buried, I had not prepared myself at all. As I walked down the aisle I wanted to scream, I wanted to say 'you can't leave me' but nothing came out, the world was spinning and I could not seem to see, I was blinded. All I remember is my father holding me up and walking me out, he did not let go of me, he let me sob into his shoulder at the grave side. When the time came for me to walk over to your grave and throw some soil onto the box that held your body, I knew you were gone. I felt it was a pointless and meaningless act where the benefits seemed fruitless.

Of course, at the wake people sent their condolences, said how well I had done, how they wanted to clap for the words I had spoken. I smiled and gave concern for their own grief, gave the answers to any questions that they asked. The offers of help in anything I might need were given in their hundreds.

Then, it was over.

The rambling diary entries of when it's all over. When you think the journey will finally become easier but actually you couldn't have been further from the truth:

12ᵗʰ April 2012

It's made me wonder what I should do next with my life. Each day seems that I am just surviving to get to the next without a plan or thought for what the future has to hold. You know me, I always liked a plan, our bucket list, my to-do lists, the wish list for things for the house that we would plan to buy, but now it all seems pointless with no meaning.

Everyone was so kind at the funeral it was difficult to get round everyone. They all said, 'If there is anything I can do just call me'. I wonder if they really mean it though. People will carry on with their everyday routines but how can I when I am just surviving each day with no reason to look forward? I could travel the world but it all seems pointless without you, even though I know you would be there in spirit. If I do call these people who have offered their support, what can they do for me, meet me for a drink? Go out for tea? None of this will bring you back to me so what would be the point but just to get me out of the house I guess, to get me off the sofa, to stop the tears.

After you died I have felt you with me, but since

the funeral you are no longer with me telling me what to do as you were when I was asking you for your final wishes. Although I am not crying uncontrollably anymore the thoughts of you are blurry, messages from you unclear.

I stayed with your family last night and I felt so disconnected from them. I don't see or feel you in them, I don't feel they understood what you would have liked or not liked from your funeral. Your name is barely mentioned, not disrespectfully but in a way that they just can't grieve for you, if they mention you they might crack. I know your ex-wife and I will speak of you often, friends will write on your wall to you still. I have lost you and need you to come back to me to guide me on where to go next.

My life needs to change. Please guide me to make this happen.

13rd April 2012

It's all going to get messy with the legal stuff, I see the turmoil it will have and to be fair any help I try to offer will be misinterpreted. I know you would want me to tell them what you would like to happen, but I am sorry I cannot, as they will make out like I have some ulterior motive and I don't want to bring more upset to myself. I know you understand but I am still sorry I cannot see your wishes through. I know you wanted to be cremated but again I couldn't change that for you my darling, it was requested, but you did get the send off you wanted so that's a compromise in a crap situation.

14th April 2012

I feel you guiding me. When I am at home I speak to you so I do not lose you, rambling as I do about the day to day, I talk as if you are still here. I have become scared that if I stop speaking to you you may leave me as you might just get bored of the silence of the house.

15th April 2012

I wrote on your wall after the funeral as people have been saying goodbye to you there.

"You can wait your whole life to find love and we

found ours. My heart never saw happiness before you. I forgave the time because of you. With you I forgot my pains, I forgot with you my misery, as I know life has breathed a little easier because you have lived.

My darling, your day yesterday was pretty much everything you wanted, thank you for giving me the strength to tell our story that you always wanted to shout from the rooftops when you were alive, I think everyone will appreciate their life a little more as it is clear that life is just a door to which love is the key. You were so much more than most people ever knew. I know you would want to thank everyone for the support that came from all corners of the world, in every medium and from so many. Like all great chapters of a book, you read it, remember it and hope the rest of the book will be the same; please give me guidance for the rest of my chapters as I am not sure where I go when I've had the best, you changed the way I think about life. Thank you my darling for a life changing chapter, as we said you are my love, sat atop the pedestal that you so justly deserve. My final goodbye to you yesterday was my saddest day, as I can barely hear your voice as I could on the days before. So it is time I say Goodbye my love, stand easy and you can now have the peace that you wished for on that barge. :) x Our song on your wall forever, it's what you said we were."

Chapter Four

The other side.

17th April 2012

Things have gotten pretty bad. I am desperate.

You said that we would grow old together, but you have gone and it now makes me change all the thoughts on life I once had and the plans that I may make seem to hold a different context. I cannot truly understand the 'where have you gone?' question that I keep asking over and over and over again, until I go there myself. God, I wish I could go there myself. I wish I could walk into the white space that I dream of, the place I think you are, peacefully waiting for me. I wish I could sink into you again.

The enormity of the funeral and the day you died plays over in my mind like a movie, but why should I have such sadness when actually now you are free, you are free from the rat race and the guilt of life's mistakes won't consume you anymore. So what happens to the soul? I have been reading books on religion wondering what has become of you now, listening to you talking to me, going to a spiritualist to get a message that might lessen the burden that sits with me since your loss.

One lady I met put one hand on mine, looked me in the eye and slowly and memorably said, "When someone is in your heart, they're never truly gone. They can come back to you, even at unlikely times." I suspect coming back is considerably harder than the ease of her words suggest. How do you pop back to me? How do you allow yourself to feel the pain of everything you must miss too? Maybe you don't miss it, maybe you like it more there, wherever there is. God I want to hold you, I want to fix it, change fate and have you home.

Generally everyone seems to have drawn the same conclusion that you are happy, they say you are at peace. The church says you are at peace anyway, the Buddhists say you pass over after 45 days, which to me seems to be a long time to be hanging around waiting. You will become another person in another era, but how do they know, how will anyone ever know? We will only ever know when it's too late to tell the story. How do we know that whatever we choose to believe on earth doesn't indeed happen? If you believe in nothing then nothing happens, if you believe that the fairies take you to a land where chocolate grows from the trees and love is currency then maybe that is what happens. Who am I to say, or any religion or person to tell you any different?

22nd April 2012

It is the 22nd of April and I have not written for so long. A sea of people hugging me out of misplaced feelings and intensity has caused the waves of grief to come when I least expect. I know you are in a better place, somewhere calmer and peaceful as you would have wished, but I miss your body by my side. The funeral was just a few weeks ago, it was everything you asked for, the memory boards of your life laid out in the village hall, people talked of the generosity and cheekiness that summed you up so well. More memories of the day return as time goes on. I did my speech as you wanted me to, to tell the world about you and the love we had, I know you loved the world to know about how wonderful you were to me so I told them everything in my heart, but there were a thousand stories I could have told if only there enough time. I know you are no longer connected to your body but when they took the coffin it felt like they were taking you away from me. Like a part of my soul exited my body with you.

I wonder if, because I was so strong when I did your speech, it might have belittled the love we had, that I should have broken down to prove how much we meant to each other. Really only you knew what we truly had and now you are gone. My dad cried with me by the side of the coffin. I felt you were standing next to me in the church, you gave me strength.

Friday 28ᵗʰ April

Five weeks has passed since you died, I float through with little knowledge or direction. I spent the day sleeping and reading at Grandad's on his green sofa as the sun came through the French windows and kept me warm. I have come to question the reason for life, it plays over in my mind, I feel on the edge of shouting at people when they talk about things I don't want to hear, people annoy me because I want to be with you. I can barely speak your name, it brings me anxiety. When you first left I felt the pain you would have had in your heart, and I do still get it every so often but not all the time any more. The back pain you used to suffer I now get most days. It's like I have connected to you, I'm now empathetic to the physical pains which plagued you.

Saturday 29th April

I feel I have changed the fundamentals of me, I don't feel myself anymore. I go upstairs and chat with a friend, telling her that maybe some grief counselling will help, it was all wrong, wrong person, wrong time and all just wrong.

Miss you.

I realised this morning that the 'I love you' that we verbalised each night and that I continued actually stopped after only two days and I haven't said it since. I feel bad for that and it is then that I realise just how bad I feel. I think the biggest revelation is that I need to find out who I am and that brings me great sadness, it should really be enlightening and wonderful but it doesn't feel that way.

I don't know what to do. Should I go for a walk, should I just lie on the floor and stay there until I disappear into the white space to come and find you? I don't know what to do, please guide me, I can't hear you since the funeral. I keep writing about you, my speech was so lovely about you, the words on your wall so wonderful about you and I have just realised that I know it all to be true - don't get me wrong - but I think that by saying it all it will bring you back to me. I'm saying it for an effect, that the effect will be that you come back to life. I have never been in a situation where I can't right a wrong through love but this time it just isn't working.

Today is shit.

Sunday 30th April/Monday 1st May

Spent time with your ex-wife and son. We set off lanterns, one landed in the tree at the church yard and we all laughed and ran off, it felt like some sort of relief. I think that it was ok to laugh, suddenly I felt for just a moment I could go back to a time before you left. When we went to the pub the landlord was talking about how people can overstep the mark, how you can put your hand over the line but you should never step over. It was strange because your ex got goose bumps, even though whatever he was talking about had no context to what we were thinking. I was a weird moment that I didn't really understand but it felt relevant. Nothing much feels relevant anymore.

When your son was leaving the farm he cried as much as he did when we took him back home some six months ago. I could not contain my tears as I watched him so upset, as we sat by your grave it felt like the end again.

Tuesday 2nd May

I've been to the doctors, the post-mortem hasn't come through to them yet and I want to know why. What could I have done, how could I have stopped this pain, how could I have saved you?

I sit there and tell the doctor I can't cope anymore, tears streaming down my face. I know I must sound like such a bore saying the same thing over and over again, but it's true - I just don't know what to do, I don't want to live without you. I want to be with you so very much. The doctors say they cannot help, that there is nothing they can do for me other than offer me some tablets. No tablets will take away this pain. I'm not depressed, I don't need another thing to battle, I'm just completely and utterly bereft; so sad I can't even put it into words. He said he didn't have any tablets for that.

Grief counselling is done by a charitable organisation and isn't usually done until after 6 months but he gave me the number anyway. He said they were all shocked to hear in the surgery of your passing and felt terrible for the loss. I wonder if they feel as bad as me, how can you ever tell what someone else feels? Maybe someone who only met you once feels as terrible as me. You can never know what someone else feels can you? I wish you could respond, I wish I could hear your voice.

I called work in the evening and agreed I would

come into the office for half an hour on Friday to see how it goes and see everyone in the first instance. I think about the last conversation you had with me, your last ever words. I can see myself stood in that office when I heard them, when I spoke with you and I feel the pain already before I have even gone in and wonder if I will be strong enough to deal with that memory every day.

The vicar wrote back to my request for support.

[Some weeks pass by -]

Day seem to turn to night and night to day, and I have lost all concept of time. I measure life by how long you've been gone. I hate that you left me like this but I feel bad for even thinking it, let alone putting it on paper as it is you that has suffered. Life seems pointless, what is the point in having things, what is the point in planning for tomorrow? People say to me that it won't go away but it will get easier, but how does it get easier if it doesn't go away? I need it to be erased from my mind to get over this loss. If this is not the worst pain that I am to experience then I want to give up now as I can not imagine going through anything worse than this.

The world keeps turning, people eat and sleep and feel ease from my words at the funeral and I only feel immensely worse that we had it all one morning and then you were gone and now just your slippers remain by the front door.

I spent time today crying into the floor as I can
barely hold myself up.

Wednesday 18th May

Mum and dad came to see me for a few hours, but the house seems sacred, I have become obsessive about what goes where in the house, who comes and goes. I can't bear for things to change. I cannot explain it but I feel I am a different to the person I once was; I don't feel I know myself, the meaning of it all, the worth of myself.

Thursday 19th May

The doctor rang to say that the post mortem had come through and that you had an artery that was 80% blocked, and as none of your other arteries were blocked you probably would never have known. Your blood pressure would have read as normal as the blood was finding other routes to go through. It may not have even come up on a cholesterol test. It makes me think of what you said when you were 19, that you would die at 43 and that you had told me that you would die young. Was it that you knew you would die, you wished it upon yourself? The cosmic ordering book says that there is something called 'natural justice'. People who step beyond the boundaries of what is okay find the cosmos has a way of catching up with them, regardless of whether the law ever does. But it happens automatically, through the individual's own process. Someone who knows they have been bad carries that knowledge with them in their heart everywhere they go, through everything that they do and eventually, one way or another, it gets to them. I don't get it though, I know you weren't faithful in the past, maybe you would get upset at people, but I didn't think you were that bad or worthy of death. You had finally found yourself, but is it then too late if you have already wished for it? But what about me? I am sure I didn't wish it, I didn't ask the cosmic order for this pain or for you to have it, I wished for us to be together in this life forever. Should I feel resentment that you did this to me?

Friday 20th May

I go around the house like you are moving me as your puppet, as I try to get ready to go to a grief counselling drop in. The tears are uncontrollable this morning as I feel your loss like a bullet in the heart, it is heavy and cannot be moved. I go to work and cry as I look out of the window I was standing at when we had our last conversation.

It plays over and over in my mind every day. It's like the proverbial broken record that I can't reach out and stop.

I bought a walkman today to listen to the psychic reading, it was £18, I am sure they were cheaper when they were popular, maybe things are cheap when they are in high demand.

I realise now that you used to open and close all the curtains and blinds in the morning and at night, it feels strange for me to be doing them. I didn't even know you were doing them, I was so lost in my world that I had stopped seeing.

I've seen Wales so many mornings across the beach as the sun makes it shimmer, I cannot pass the window without looking out along the beach.

The bedding I cannot bring myself to change but I know I need to wash it soon, but how will I? It, along with your unwashed clothes. They hold the last smell of you, I can barely think about it. The pillow case for anyone else would smell horrible, but I loved your smell, even your sweaty smell, which you could never understand.

Saturday 21st May

The sun has been shining so brightly this morning, I felt the coil of grief tighten up inside me as the morning went on. Then the heavens opened and the rain came down - is that you telling me that you are as sad as me? Or is it just some freak weather pattern? I am so desperate for messages from you that take hope from everything I can find.

I wish you would come back, I cannot bear the thought that you are not here, it seems like a lifetime since you held me and the pictures seem so far away. Days don't pass like they used to, they pass in a way I cannot explain and would wish upon no person.

Sunday 22nd May

Did you turn the TV on overnight, I definitely turned it off and when I came down it was playing, did you do it to tell me you are here? I feel shit this morning, I am angry that the rest of the world carries on, I am angry that everyone is so happy in their lives and I don't have you to be happy with, I can't get into my head that you are gone.

Had sugar puffs this morning, you always said it makes your wee smell of sugar and it did, but since you died it hasn't, strange hey?

Mum calls me each day and I cry down the phone to her. I tell her every time that I want you back and she tells me she's sorry she can't do anything. I hope you will hear me and come home to me.

Packed the washing away. I think of you all the time, I move around with little purpose. Not sure I want to go to work tomorrow, think I'd rather just stay in the house with you. Think I will hand my notice in, I know you are telling me just get another job first, but I can't. I have thought a lot today about what you would do - you told me so often that you would not survive without me. I never dreamed it would be you, you made me so cautious not to leave you alone in life I just didn't imagine it would be you leaving me.

I feel you showing me a more positive light to all this and it keeps creeping through. Don't give up showing me because I will see it fully soon. Don't give up on helping me through this.

Tuesday 24ᵗʰ May

Called the doctors yesterday and they have booked me in again, they said they need to support me more as I cried hysterically down the phone. She asked me if I had been thinking of ending my own life. I really do think that is the most ridiculous question, anyone that doesn't think that they would rather be dead along with their partner, is simply lying. I told her that too. Of course I'd rather be with you, wherever you are resting, to find peace, light and love. But I know that is not my fate, that I have to suffer through this however it ends.

Went onto the beach, cried and cried, there was a man there walking his dogs and although he could not see me crying he kept looking over at me. I wondered if you were in him somehow, the soul of you, how did he know? Probably because I was so slumped in my walk. I felt he wanted to ask if I was alright, I wondered how I would tell him: my partner died, he died and now I sit on the beach without him, with only one shadow showing on the sand and it makes me so sad... two months and one day and I feel worse each day. How would I tell a complete stranger that? I know I couldn't have just said 'yeah I'm alright' because that is definitely not the case. In truth though, that is exactly what I would have done, and I probably would have smiled when I said it.

Been writing to people to say thank you for their

support as didn't get time in the beginning because there were just too many. I need to make myself a food diary of things I should eat each day to keep weight on as it's falling off and it will annoy me when someone mentions it.

My toes have been cold since you left, I had noticed it but hadn't told you until now. I miss you warming them for me.

I can hear a police siren - or is it an ambulance? - I pray no one has to go through what we have gone through.

I have been angry today, I have hated you today for leaving me like this, it is cruel.

Your work called me. I have offered to speak to some of your work colleagues. I thought those who went on the cycle ride might be suffering with guilt and grief. I don't know, maybe they don't care but I offered to talk to them about the circumstances and what actually happened to your heart in the hope that it might give comfort to anyone who's grieving. If they had been with you maybe you would have felt embarrassed, maybe you would not have had your final conversation with me, maybe I would not have been the last person you spoke to.

I feel worse as I told you'd be fine when you were already knackered. I wish I had told you to stop, maybe you would be with me now. Did I tell you what was wrong with you? Your ventricle was 80% blocked with build up and the blood clot could not pass through. The reason you did not have any other heart pain was because the rest of the arteries were ok. I feel you carried around the weight of guilt in your heart and it built up. No, I did tell you that already didn't I? I am a little bit crazy at the moment.

I have been reading loads. They say the soul is in the heart, which would make sense as to why you got a heart condition and never knew. You always felt an unsettled soul, you had foreseen your own death when you were younger and allowed guilt and a painful childhood to never be discussed and that sat heavy on your heart until your final year, but then I fear it was too late to mend.

Wednesday 26th May

I didn't write to you yesterday, it was a write off, no words can even explain how it went. Today I went for an interview, I went to call you, to tell you how it had gone and realised I couldn't. I didn't know who to call then because nobody I called would compare to telling you about it.

Did you love me? I don't know now, so much time has gone by and I worry that maybe we didn't have everything like I thought. Everyone keeps saying they feel you with them in their dreams and in their presence, why can't I? Did I do something wrong, say something wrong that made your spirit leave me? I am sorry if I did, I just need you to tell me where you have gone, I need you so much I would move to the end of the earth if I thought I could find you to hold me just one more time, to feel your lips touch mine, just one more time. I would disappear into the white space of beyond if I knew that was where you were. Please, it's too much for my heart to take. I watch as my heart beats harder through my chest each day that passes, as if it is inevitably going to fall out and be rescued by you.

Thursday 27th May

Managed to get onto the beach which feels like something I haven't managed to do for so long, but I have no concept of time any more, so who am I to say?

I had been reading last night about past life regression and I had a dream about you. I haven't felt quite as alone as I have previously. I dreamt we had a house that was built in seconds, it was a flat pack type house but was built with real beauty with plants hanging from the porch and lots of light and glass, but with an age to it that gave it character. The front was a summer type house, conservatory style. The neighbours had come round and said we couldn't have the house there as it was blocking their view, but it was attached and in front of another large building in the forest, but also in the city. You were just there in the dream, around all the time, it gave me such peace within the dream, it was wonderful. It was like it was before when just your presence gave me strength. I forgot that.

I got the job babes, the recruitment lady was so happy. I felt better to take the job as I had handed my notice in at the other, I didn't feel like I was cheating them. Heard back from one of druid guys I've been messaging. They have a pretty nice view on where you are.

Bought a kindle so I can look into all of the past life

books and hypnosis things that you seem to have been willing me to read. I feel my heart and back aching again today, I feel it is you, you are telling me something, I will await for further signs of what that is. I feel I am starting to come to terms with things, that actually I was meant to be here for you. I had become your teacher and to rest your soul; you were here to make me realise what I always knew but hadn't done anything about, that I have more about me than I am actually fulfilling, something more spiritual and creative. I can offer the world more than I have, and I should be as this is my true role. The book that I read has stopped any fear I had of death.

Chapter Five

Acceptance.

Seven months later… 28th November.

Seven months has passed and time seems to have gone by without me writing to you - it doesn't mean I haven't thought of you but I have tried to push on with life. It's now eight months since you died and I can barely breathe without you, it is like you left so long ago but only yesterday. It's as though I had a dream that you died and I am still trying to get used to it. I try to wish for you back to me but I can't make it happen and I feel frustrated. I just want life to go back to normal. I don't want to have to think and do things to make myself feel better, I just want to see your face. Your birthday is looming and I want you to be here so that I can spoil you. I start to think maybe I just didn't spoil you enough, if I could have you back for one more day I could be sure that I would make you know how loved you were. You went so quickly I didn't get a chance to make sure you knew, that you really knew. I see your face as you lay there on that fateful day, and I remember the love that filled me at the thought of everything that you were, and now I just miss that love. I look at pictures and my heart feels as though it is being squeezed dry. I still wish you had done things that were really annoying because at least then there would be something I could be grateful that I didn't need to put up with anymore.

Now seems the right time to get moving on the bucket list. I had not wanted to look at it but now it seems to be my saviour.

I've decided to stop writing to you for now. It doesn't mean I don't care, but when I forget to write I feel such unbelievable guilt and I don't need another thing to feel guilt for. So I'll just carry you around in my heart, so you can see it all for yourself, you can feel what I feel.

The summary of year 1:

23rd March 2012 - 23rd March 2013

I lived the first year in a bubble, in some ways. Although I didn't realise it at the time, I lived with him in my head and very little existed outside of that. There is a movie called *Truly, Madly, Deeply* which, I think, would stand as a very good summary of my relationship with Ben that year; a strange half-reality where he still existed but only in my head. The more normal that became, the more I accepted this as part of my daily life, the more the edges of fantasy and reality would blur into an indistinguishable whole. The first anniversary was spent in a daze. I had previously found that compartmentalization was a useful tool to get over most things in life: job doesn't work out, box the disappointment; shelve it, get a new one. The boy that you love doesn't love you back: box him up, stick him up on the proverbial shelf and move on. When grief came knocking the usual tactics were destined to fail. The box just wasn't big enough, it was spilling out all over the place and the shelf would never take its weight. The proverbial was going to hit the fan and I knew my default tactics were no match for what was to come.

I spent most of the early part of the year bargaining. Just one more day, if I can just turn back time I will give up everything. I would exist with nothing else but him if you let me have him for one more day. I'm not sure who my cries were reaching and I will never know until I too reach the end of my life, if in fact anyone heard them at all. If there is nothing at the end, no bright white light, no meeting of lost souls, then there will be no 'ah-ha' moment where all of the strange coincidences, the feeling that hc was there and the cries to something greater will suddenly make themselves clear. There will be just nothing.

In fact, I became desperate for coping mechanisms. I needed to find a way through the physical and emotional turmoil of grief. I have seen people lie by the grave, unable to move from the floor, the bed, just existing and, for some, that is a way to cope. My way, in those early days, was to write down everything that happened. I campaigned and organised things in his memory. I talked about him to everyone, and everything would always revert back to him in every story I had to tell. It made people uncomfortable by the end of the first year but they knew it would be indecent to do anything else but accept it or choose to avoid me.

I pushed to organise an event on the first year of his anniversary, to redo the cycle ride that was never finished. We did it in aid of Comic Relief this time and not Sports Relief, which was the chosen charity the year he died. It made people uncomfortable, but I persevered regardless.

I climbed Kilimanjaro in his memory, started to do

things from the bucket list. Started to learn photography and set this up as a little business with a website, it was something I could do while I isolated myself from the world. I read entire books in just an evening and did exactly what I was able to manage. Everything else I was sure to dismiss.

I did, however, manage to achieve the following things from the bucket list in year 1:

1. I climbed Kilimanjaro as I mentioned, through group effort nearly £14k was raised.

2. I went to Australia and travelled the gold coast.

3. I went to Spain.

4. I took up photography.

More impressively, I attended weddings. Weddings are hard and underestimated as an achievement for a grieving widow type.

The summary of year 2:

23rd March 2013 – 23rd March 2014

Going into year two was much more about survival - not like the early days, better than that, but survival through finding focus and meaning where there had previously been none. I had to stop fearing stuff, it was not helpful. I had made such progress and I'd learnt that there was no specific grieving pattern I had gone through. When I was going through it, I didn't feel as though I passed between the typical stages of denial, anger, bargaining, or acceptance - or certainly not in any uniform order. I felt that my grief was much more complex. I felt annoyed that this momentous, life changing event might be summarised in just four emotions. People like a pattern, a pathway in all walks of life, grief included. Acceptance was not real, it was not what grief looked like at all - not to me, anyway. Yet when I look back to it, when I read about the cycle of grief, when I read through my own diary, that is exactly what happened. I did follow a pattern of sorts.

The second anniversary was much less published. It was no longer a celebration of Ben, but a 'time to move on'. People ignored his memory at the Sports Relief event and struggled to even acknowledge I was there. I had taken my mother, so I just held my head up high and carried on. People didn't want to be reminded and to be honest, now I know what I know about how long no one noticed he wasn't there with the rest of the riders, I understand the level of guilt that people must carry.

I had not known a lot about that day and how it played out, I only had the information from the paramedic, just desperate to know whether he had died in pain, what his likely last moments would have been like. Could I have done something different? I just hoped it was painless. Had I known he'd been left while they carried on to two more stop points before calling to tell me he was no longer with them, the guilt of the event organisers would not only be understandable but inevitable.

The company who organised the cycle ride had always tried to keep Ben's death a low key thing, a note of condolence in the paper being the very corporate start and end point. It became quite clear they did not want to remember what had happened, as to do that would be to keep the events of that day fresh in people's minds, maybe leading to the arrival of lawyers and a lengthy - and costly - lawsuit over the safety of the event, dragging the Sports Relief name with them as they did so.

This year, I discovered that grief changes the shape of relationships and seeks out those who have no foundation to stand alone. This was the year I started to walk away from the friendships I had previously held so dear. It was the year I said, 'I will no longer continue to give of myself to those who do not appreciate it'. I looked at friendships and asked myself what we had in common, was I making them a better person or was I too reliant on them. I made some valuable, yet quick and severe changes to my personal tribe.

Bucket list items completed:

1. Went to Chicago.

2. Set up Sunshine People as an ongoing cause.

3. Went to a festival as a punter.

4. Completed a 5k fun run.

5. Volunteered for Barnardo's.

6. Completed a sculpture course.

The summary of year 3:

March 2014 – 2015 – Year 3

When the Korean war happened, some 60 years ago, it tore entire families apart. As the country divided into north and south so too did its people. Younger generations of a family may never have met, may never have even known of the existence of other members of their own family as time and memory erased the past. Nowadays they have planned reunions. These reunions last just three days before each party must return to their respective side of the partition. Of course, the moment of reunion must be amazing - but the goodbye must be like the start of grief all over again, not knowing whether that was your final farewell. And as the end of your own life moves closer, bathed in the shadow of a life that might have been, that feeling of loss must inevitably grow until you wonder, perhaps it would have been better had we never met at all. If today I was offered three more days with Ben, I would take them in a heartbeat. But I also know that the grief of the goodbye would shatter me; I would not be stronger and wiser a second time around. I would have to die with him a second time. But I would still take those three days regardless.

People see the strength, they see the things that I am doing in his memory, that I still talk with love for him, but I would give up all of that - all that I have become - just be with him for one more day.

What this year brought was love; my heart got bigger for everything and everyone. I allowed myself to love and in turn I realised that I was not only living for him but also for myself.

Bucket list items completed:

1. Parkinson's Charity walk - we raised £2k.

2. Machu Picchu.

3. Climbed Snowdon.

4. Became an approved foster carer.

The summary of year 4:

March 2015 – 2016 – year 4

In Ben's memory on the anniversary of his passing in March 2016, I wrote this blog as I sat in India.

This week will mark the 4th year without having Ben in my life. Wow, it hurts when you put it like that, but in truth grief does truly ease if you want it to. You can choose to allow the grief to swallow and consume you or you can say, I will be a stronger and a better human for this loss of the person who has passed.

Either you choose to take the all-consuming pain and turn it into something better, kinder, stronger and worthy of the grief that consumes you, or you say, I'm going to ask the world for sympathy. When I post or blog or talk of Ben and my grief, I never ask for sympathy, I only ask that you will take the experience and learn from it. That you will never take life or love for granted, that you will live each day as it could be your last, that you will take a chance in love. Do it because you are strong, because you heard this story and realised life is really too short for anything else. Life is not for second chances, it's not for, 'I wish I had' and 'I'm sorry I never said', you should say how you feel because even though you may put your heart on the line, it is better than arriving at your final day saying, 'I adored but I never said.'

It is true that a part of you dies, a fictitious limb is missing at the loss of a loved one, but it is your choice what you replace it with. When I say replace, I do not mean 'forget' or 'move on' or any of the other silly phrases people use, I mean, fill the gap by continuing to carry the good of them within your heart in all that you do. In the last four years I have been living life with an open heart but not loving with an open heart. There is a very big difference, as I have recently discovered. I have that now and am looking forward to a year where I put my heart on the line, allow it to be rejected and broken and say that's OK. I have so many times in the last year said something in my mind to Ben that if someone heard would stare at me open mouthed and in shock for several minutes. He knew me and I knew him, so much so that there was nothing that could not be said between us. I have feared to be that person, feared of loss and heartbreak. Now though I know that I need to do all of that for my soul to continue to grow, and to be true to myself. If being true to oneself cannot be accepted by those around you or who are party to it, they are quite simply the wrong people.

I have seen death close up, heard my love's last words and for that I have chosen to never say no to life. To say I will live like it will be my last breath, that if my last words were to be uttered there would never be undercurrents of regret. I live for others who can't be here, grateful to breathe, mindful not to waste the privileges of being born with opportunities that allow me to travel, to form worldwide friendships, the knowledge at our fingertips and the possibility to do good is easy. This blog is for you my darling, who I never need to move on from, just ensure I am true to myself and continue to love open heartedly those around me, as I did with you.

In November 2015 I travelled around the world, where I met a tall handsome American man in Santa Barbara who had approached me in a bar as I sat writing a blog. I'm not sure whether I was overly attracted to him in the first instance, but we agreed to go on a date the following night and then I had planned to leave the following day to continue to travel up Route 1 of the Pacific highway. What came about was a change of plans, in that I ended up staying in Santa Barbara for the following four days where we spent time together in a whirlwind romance. It taught me how closed I had been when I thought I had been so open and how wonderful it would be to be open to love once again. He too learnt things in our time together, but that is his story and not mine to share. I had forgotten what it felt like to be so comfortable in the company of another human, physically, without being lost in longing, emotion and fear of being broken by the end of it. He came to spend two more days with me further up the coast and although we had known each other for so little time it was like we had known each other our whole lives in some ways. Another visit back to him a month later and we were to eventually confirm that while we had felt a connection so strong it was impossible to ignore, it was also a meeting that was only intended to help us learn lessons and move ourselves on in our individual journeys, just not together. It was a hard lesson for me, but one that I came out of stronger and started to see the world a little differently - not badly, just differently.

It taught me I had been living and loving a ghost, a ghost who may love me but could now not show me what love was.

Bucket list items completed:

1. Bought a house.

2. Moved from the cottage by the sea.

3. Went to Chicago.

4. Went to Denver, Colorado.

5. Drove up the Pacific Highway.

6. Went to Hong Kong.

7. Went to India to ride the trains.

Chapter Six

Understanding.

Grandad

Love, loss and death was not to just to be confined to my soulmate in those five years, it was also to stretch out to my dear grandfather. It taught me the depth and breadth of love and loss and how differently it can happen. How if we are open to the moments they can change our lives, they can makes us more mindful and stronger than we even aspired to be.

I guess that by the time my grandad had reached his nineties, the year that Ben died, he had already started to deteriorate but he was still functioning so well that it was difficult to tell. He was giving lifts to the equally old but less able, for the market or other such luncheon clubs. He continued to sort the chickens and the many tasks involved on my dad's small holding that he tended to and that he came to love so much. So often being at my parents house so early in the morning he would wake them to ask what he was due to do for the day. My dad was not only a son to him but he had now become his best friend and his carer. I would do the background admin of direct debits and changing insurances, but it was my parents that took care of the day-to-day. Grandad was the everyday presence in their lives. My grandfather's hearing had been poor since I had known him, we put this down to his time in the coal mines, but it meant telephone calls were impossible. He had suffered illness in this time and when my grandmother went into a care home because of her dementia he was racked with guilt as he felt he should have continued to care for her, but after she had gotten up in the night and fallen and broken her arm, his deafness came to haunt him as he had not heard her. He sat up with her all night until he was able to ring my dad at a reasonable time to ask for help. It was only then that she went into a home. She was often scared of everything, including her own family. After a year at the care home and just three months after Ben died, she suffered a heart attack too.

It was the day of my grandmother's funeral. I loved her as my grandmother but there was very little connection to her at the end, she had always been a generous lady and was a wonderful grandmother, but I was always aware she had not been able to love wholeheartedly and it had made those around her a little sad. I read a poem at the funeral, for my dad more than anything, to support him as he was the only one to read. His words struck me most when he said, 'my mother chose well when she chose my father'. It had been very true after 70 years of marriage.

I got into the car and wept and wept, not for my grandmother because she was now freed from the immense fear and the unknown that the dementia gave her - in truth I had not seen her for a year, she struggled with visitors and so my father made sure it was just him, at a regular time each week in the end - but I wept for how much I missed Ben. I felt selfish for it, but it just came and I let it, I let myself weep until there was nothing left. My mother just sat there in silence, she let me cry and it was just what I needed, she put a hand on me and when I was done, she asked if I wanted her to drive and I said it was ok and we drove back in the silence of our own thoughts.

My grandfather had a good few years with my dad, just the two of them, not having the sickening worry for Nana anymore. Just the two of them being best mates and doing what they loved to do: build things, make fires, grow things and mostly be in each others company.

My grandfather's deterioration had been so very slight over the ensuing few years, it was only when he was hit by a severe case of gastroenteritis that he failed to fully recover. As my grandfather was recovering from his illness we were, at the same time, planning a surprise party for my father's 70th birthday in the September; a month earlier than his actual birthday, but that was mainly for the weather - and also so as not to give the game away. My grandad did not know until the day of the party. He was so deaf and still recuperating, so we didn't want there to be any confused conversations, misheard words, or any other incident where my grandfather might inadvertently let the secret slip.

So I went down to see my grandfather on the day of the party. Whenever my grandfather opened the door to someone he would always have a look on his face of complete joy to see them. He had this way of making you feel like the most special person that ever existed in all the world. So anyway, when I arrived and he gave me hugs and kisses and I told him the plan, he wept because he was so happy that my father was getting this done for him. I realised he saw himself as the main friend in my dad's life, as he saw him every day and never saw any of the other connections that my father had. He felt pleased that his son was loved, and that love existed. I didn't ask him about his tears as I felt I understood them well enough. Then suddenly my father arrived in his beekeeping suit, in an old clapped-out car that made a racket only I could hear.

'Oh hello, what are you doing here?' (he had not known I was visiting in Dorset).
'Oh just up with grandad for the day.'
'Oh, ok.' He looks at grandad.
'So dad, wanna come off to look at the queens?'(He is a beekeeper!)
'No not today son.'
'Yeah, and I'm here dad,' I said. 'Besides, mum said you are off to a BBQ.'
'Oh, I'm not too worried.'
'Well you should probably get back and have a wash', I said, as the sweat stuck to this forehead from all the physical work he had done that morning.

As my dad walked out, my grandad gave me a wink and a wry smile - a look I will never forget.

My dad's birthday was a roaring success. Friends came from every era of his lifetime, those he had worked with all over the world, those from his youth and local friends. When he walked in, his face was a picture and he could not understand what was happening. Grandad wept again, because he loved his son and loved that his son was loved, all the work that my mother had done to make it happen was admired by him.

His decline was pretty rapid after that. He was unable to walk but his mind was active and I spent my weekends with them, my weeknights too when possible, offering my support. As well as being his primary carer my father was also my grandad's interpreter, as grandad could really only hear my dad and me - something to do with the tone of our voices, I presumed.

I was able to envisage the future and what that was going to look like with regards to his care and imminent death. I have wondered as to, should I have had to care for Ben, what I would have done. No one wants to hear it though. They can't face the reality that the death of someone in that situation needs to be clinically thought through. If you do not put them first, you will only project it onto the very person who already has their own stuff to deal with as the end of their days draws nearer. You cannot show them your tears. I could have cried when I fed my grandfather knowing he had only a few days left, but I smiled at him always.

At the end, after spending so many years being his rock, my father realised the loss of not only his father but his best mate was imminent. I had offered to take over the role of primary carer, as I felt I was able to do this in a more systematic way with no emotion at this point. After all, it was really only helping my grandfather get over his final hurdle. My grandfather and I had talked in detail about his death and his beliefs over the years. I knew what he wanted and that he was more concerned about everyone else. He needed to not have their concerns upon him at that moment. I made sure I reassured him in those final weeks as I helped my father nurse him that I was okay as I felt that he was most concerned for me after losing Ben and seeing my grief in all its depth.

My father had spent several weeks getting my grandfather into the car in the morning, and bringing him to their house, where he would sit him in front of the fire. However he was starting to get uncomfortable even being able to do this, and one day when he had said he was ready to go home his shoes would no longer fit back on him, his feet had swollen so much in just the time he had been there. My father took off his own slippers, put them on his father and walked out barefoot to the car, as he knew that granddad had wanted so desperately to get back home. My father was not even aware of his actions that evening.

A few days later it was the weekend, and so I was there for my weekend visit. It was a Sunday and grandad's catheter had become blocked; it had happened before, but we knew it could be fatal. He was showing signs of possible infection and if it could not be cleared soon it might back up and burst his bladder. We were desperately calling the standard emergency lines, my father's anxiety was growing, grandad could barely be moved and we paced up and down desperately wondering what we should do. I tried to keep Dad calm but he felt helpless. We feared the end might come at a time that we could have prevented, and seeing grandad in so much discomfort was adding to the pain. My Dad went back to granddad and had an idea; he decided to bang the tube between two fists, and it started to flow again as the the blockage became free. My father wept and wept. I would later realise that it was the only time I would cry over my grandfather's passing. The image will stay with me forever as my grandfather, so exhausted, held his son's shoulder in thanks and lay down and slept for the next 12 hours. It was an image so powerful on the journey that we take in life. Of fear, love and support, a lifetime spent together with everyone in the room knowing that the end was so near.

I asked grandad what he wanted to do: did he want me and dad to continue to care for him at home, or would he prefer to go somewhere else? He said, 'If you can do it, please can you, but if you can't I will understand and be grateful you tried'.

I responded with, 'You will not leave here, we will take care of you always, that's what we are here for.' He nodded, squeezed my hand in the lightest of ways and I continued to feed him.

He had visitors and dad and I would always be near as he had requested. I think mainly because we had come to know his code for things he needed without the use of words that had become too difficult for him now. It was a long and horrendous five days in the end, I had hoped for a more peaceful and swift end to his life. Everyone wanted to be a part of his passing and this made it more challenging for him. His senses were being awakened and torn every time he could hear anything, the worst time being when I had needed an hour's rest and my grandfather, who was heavily dosed on drugs, seemed to sense my father and suddenly started screaming that he wanted to get up over and over again. He just wanted to be with my father. I found this hard and my father was the first person I had to tell that having people in the house was not helping. My father agreed and we went about asking very disgruntled family members if they would mind leaving. It was not about me, my father or anyone else that loved him, it was about him, his wishes, his peaceful passing. Screw everyone's grief at this point! Suddenly people turn up when someone is about to die, suddenly they make the time when their offers of support are far too late to make any difference. aIt was my father, supported by my mother, who had dealt with it all for so long. I had only come in at the end to support them, and to follow my grandfather's wishes.

In the delirious small hours as I sat by his bed waiting for the end to arrive, he sat up and moaned and talked about the people he could see as he stared at the ceiling. He often fitted and I hoped that whatever was going on, that he was not in pain. I pulled out decayed skin from his mouth, as it was lying there festering and I didn't want it to choke him, even though he was hours from death. The bed that automatically turned him did not arrive before he started his medication. They felt that it would be so quick that it would be fine to not use it, but that was not the case. It would go on some five days, all the while we were unable to touch or turn him for fear of him fitting. After he went into a severe and scared state, when I had tried to move him early on in the palliative care, I prayed that I could just keep going. Help came from a Marie Curie nurse on what would turn out to be his final night. I called her the lady who brought light when there was complete darkness, and I am forever indebted to that shining light. The last 24 hours in the house, since I had asked everyone to leave was peaceful; grandad was finally peaceful and I knew that I had done right by him. So grandad was restful, he briefly and calmly looked at me, I spoke softly to him and not long after that he went into a coma. When the Marie Curie nurse came at 10pm, I had had so little sleep

I was exhausted, and all of the anxiety that I'd tried so hard to keep hidden could finally be let free.

I sat up and talked with the nurse. She talked about coming from Birmingham originally, she was a woman of faith and I felt what a great soul she was. She agreed to wake me at 5am so we could turn him again. She woke me and, as I walked into my grandad's room, she stood away from my grandfather and I saw the skeleton of a man before me. I had not noticed the state of his decline until that very moment. He had died. It was two o'clock in the morning. I let out a sigh of relief because I knew he could rest easy and he was no longer in pain. I opened the window and lit a candle, I don't know why, I just thought it would help him pass to wherever it is we go after death, and if we go nowhere as my grandad believed, then it wouldn't hurt.

I had imagined this day and wept at even the thought of it, thinking that nothing could be worse than this. But in the witching hour, the reality was just a relief that this beautifully kind man could now rest with ease.

We waited for the paramedic to come and declare the time of death, those words reminding me of Ben. So I got in the car and headed to my parents to tell them, and when I got there my mother was already awake and reading in bed. We woke my father to tell him. I told him to stay, I did not want him to see him now, he was not the man that we loved, he was not there, it was an image he did not need to take on his journey to remember him with, it is one I would prefer not to have and it did not need to be shared. I went back, took some of my mum's jam to the Marie Curie nurse, to whom no gift or words would be enough, but I guess she knew that. We dressed him and the undertakers arrived. I picked up all the paperwork, cleared my things, packed up the car, cancelled as many direct debits as I could without the certificate and left a list of things still to do with my parents. I drove home and was back by the afternoon. And then I slept.

The next day I went back to work. I still hadn't cried over the man that I could once have cried over just the thought of losing. Now I realised that the tears would just be my selfishness.

The funeral came, I wrote something I wish I hadn't shared as it was my personal moments to me and him. Sometimes there is a dignity in silence. The family ignored me and to be honest it clarified that they cared more for themselves than the man we had lost. Money became more important to them and I was glad when it was all over, to be away from the horrible selfishness. I could have my parents, who I valued and whose moral code I could follow, and I felt glad to be away from the rest.

The connection I had with my grandfather was not the same as that. We liked the same things. With him, I could sit and feel loved without saying a word. We understood each other. He told me in one of our final chats together, as we talked in our usual spot at the kitchen table until the seats became too hard for our bottoms and we needed to move to the sofa, about how he had never been able to speak to someone as he could with me, that in fact maybe he shouldn't tell me everything he did. He said that if I told anyone else his secrets he would come back to haunt me. His stories were amazing, he was funny, no one could ever fail to laugh with my grandfather around, no child could feel unloved around him. He had a look when he greeted you that I have not experienced again since he passed, one I took for granted. It was one of huge love, acceptance and gratefulness for your existence. He hid his true thoughts about things and let love shine out of him always, he was a wonder within my life that was significant for the way I lived and the morals I kept. Although my grandfather was less likely to say what he really thought, as he always liked to keep the peace, it was the only trait I was not able to adopt. I have had to speak my truths. Sorry grandad, but maybe in hindsight you wish you had done the same.

I went to the house just before it was due to be cleared. I wanted desperately to be able to cry, to let go of the grief. I have seen what it does to those who are unable to grieve, through unsaid words or bitter feelings, but nothing came. I sat on the green sofa as the light shone through the French windows and felt nothing. He was gone and I missed his presence and I wondered if, wherever he was, he was ok. I wanted nothing of my grandfather's possessions, it would never represent the connection I had with him.

It was some time after the funeral when my father gave me my grandad's wallet. It was threadbare as he was never one for wanting new things, he liked to stick with what he knew.

'You should have this', said my Father, 'it holds a note that you gave him and a photo'. I remembered him asking me for that passport photo when I had showed it to him. The note had been written after an incident when my grandmother was declining rapidly into her dementia. She was unable to leave the house and Christmas day at my parents' place was looking unlikely for my grandfather as he, understandably, did not want to leave without her. I went down to their house and managed to coax her out just long enough to enjoy the food and for my grandfather to enjoy the company of his family. I wrote my grandfather a note, 'I wanted you to know that whatever happens, however sad you feel you must remember how loved you are by me, always'. It was a bit ragged around the edges like it had been pulled out a few times. It had been treasured as it had been in there some five years. A tear came but not all of my tears.

Loss takes so many forms. The end of my grandfather's life, and Ben's, and even my grandmother's were all deaths but that is where the similarities end. The emotions, the journeys and the stories all vary. I guess you could say that powerful lessons were learnt from each of them, but even those were very different again.

With most things, particularly with death but usually with all human connection, we try to compare. It is a human trait. Our story is the same or different, our loss is greater or lesser, we coped with it better or worse.

What I have found so far in my journey is to never forget to listen, to allow people to speak, to understand that our individual stories should never be compared but just simply listened to, accepted and empathised with.

When you connect with people, it connects you to the world, it allows you to live open-heartedly. You become wiser, stronger. When those people die, the choice to open your heart wider is yours to make, but fear of heartache is, in my opinion, the greatest fear of all.

Chapter Seven

Lessons learned.

That day, the day you wake up after you lose someone, you have a moment when you forget the bad thing that's happened. And then you remember and it's like being told all over again.

'Their life has expired', what a line. A line that must haunt medical staff all over the world. The physical pain returns in many forms, physical heartache, backaches, cramps, nausea, it keeps coming. If we don't allow ourselves to feel the grief it's like a bottle of champagne that gets shaken to its core and then left. Eventually the cork will force itself out and the liquid will spill, lost forever, and you will be left with only half of yourself. Grief is not comparable, it does not follow a journey, it has no answers. If you are unprepared for the idea of dealing with it, your grief will consume you and take away any lust for life that you have within you.

I would have done anything for him, I would have taken care of his sick body or mind forever, I would have found a way to make him better if he had survived. Whatever it took, I would have done it to have him alive. That is what I wanted so I could still have him and the connection that we had. But would he have wanted the same? Would he have wanted to live in a body that did not function? In truth, that is what would have been left after such a huge heart attack. He would not have wanted that and in some ways I am glad it wasn't the case, because the emotional pain that he would have suffered could well have been worse. I once read that men cope with grief much worse than women, unable to process their feelings and guilt because they are unable to fix whatever the problem is, so the emotion eats them up. I never would have wanted him to go through that. I would never have wanted him to suffer, even though I selfishly wanted to have my final words of love with him, to hold him and know that he knew I was holding him. Grief can be selfish in those early days, but it is within your power to rationalise the anger, the selfishness and the injustice of it all.

The normal breakup of a relationship is ego driven, it is quantifiable to a certain extent. 'He doesn't love me', 'She doesn't love me', 'He changed', 'I wanted him to change'. You can go and talk it through and figure out the whys and why nots. But with grief there is nothing, there is no hurt ego that can be mended, no conversation that has the potential to heal, it's empty and gone, with no remedy.

I loved him, it's in the past tense, but why should it be, if love is to continue always? It's past because his physical presence is no longer here and in truth we do need that to truly know someone is there for you, or so it feels.

There is always a question that I am struck by which is the meaning of it all and the measuring of it. The measure of someone's life and what meaning it held. Tim Minchin once said in a graduation speech that you should not search for meaning as there is none. I tend to agree with it on one hand, but on the other I feel that each life has its own type of meaning; it is what you make it and how you measure it that ultimately counts. How many people you were able to help and what part of the world was better because of your existence? You will only be measured in truth by the people that see you for who you truly are and the heart and soul of you can only be truly seen if you love open-heartedly. It's a cycle you see, you will not realise you are loving open-heartedly until you are doing it and only then can you be measured by anyone.

The ancient Egyptians believed that in death, when the soul reached the entrance to heaven, the gods asked it two questions. The answers it gave would determine whether or not they were admitted. Those questions were: Have you found joy in your life? And has your life brought joy to others?

In my opinion, it is only once you accept death, accept that you will die, that those around you will die, that you can truly be free. We see it as morbid, but how can it be? It is inevitable. But so many of us are shocked when death occurs, myself included. I wasn't even thinking that it would happen to me or my loved ones, ever.

When death came, I found that the memories didn't come in clean lines, I got them in bits and I had to try to decipher the picture. Let me tell you something I know for sure: your perception of those moments will change. Others memories will paint a different picture dependant on your outlook on life. There is very little point in being too worried about having it all clear, it just needs to be what you make it. Whatever you hold dear in your memories, let them be loving and positive because bitterness will destroy you.

Darkness will come into our lives in many forms, we are not here to have everything rosy, you don't grow and develop that way. We do not expand our knowledge by everything working out exactly as we'd hoped, where every day we smile and laugh at the amazingness of our lives. Darkness happens, and we choose whether to make the dark into light, we choose whether to find a way through it and make ourselves greater at the end.

Of course, hindsight is a wonderful thing. 'If I had stopped it that day', 'If I'd followed my instinct', 'If I had held him tighter, begged him more to stay alive, 'told him not to go on that ride'. But you have to make a conscious choice: let that 'If only.....' destroy you, or realise that life has a path and sometimes nothing you do will change the course of it; it can be diverted, but you will always find yourself on the same road in the end.

Memories

Death changes everything. A statement of the obvious, you might say. Of course it changes things, including the perception of the person that died. They will never exist as they once did, with all their faults and imperfections. Their faults will vanish.

As I wrote this I went through old emails, texts and things I had not seen for nearly five years. My memories of the time I had with Ben was secure and safe, I forgot the passion of our arguments, I forgot how besotted I was with him and him with me, his daily photos of his life and the world as he saw it through his eyes. In grief, we change the perception of not only the situation but the person and how you ever interacted. I have seen some widows focus on only the good, as we are all guilty of putting those loved ones on a pedestal. There are also those of us who can only focus on the bad. I guess that the built-in optimist or pessimist in each of us can rule these memories too. I wept as I read through it all, for everything I had forgotten but mainly for being loved unconditionally, being loved so fiercely that the line between love and obsession was blurry, but existed regardless. We realise when they are gone how it had taken time to build the relationship that we have with our loved ones. How difficult it is to fill the hole that they left in us.

I sat in a café as I read all the history, struggling to

keep myself composed, confused by the memories and the grief. A man walked in, smiled at everyone he walked past, gave a thumbs up to me and started chatting to one lady. I chuckled because I had forgotten that is what Ben would have done. He would chat with anyone, you never wanted to get caught in a lift with him if you were a timid person, he'd have you chatting before you'd made it to the first floor. Grief and memories never stop they just change shape.

All we ever have of each other is memories, we either raise people up or knock them down. It is your choice, saint or sinner. I have learnt that we should not need to make the person either, just let them rest in a place of love and forgiveness. The world as we see it is not reality. Find the calm place in your emotions for them, no extremes, just an unconditional love and acceptance. When you find that, your grief will no longer continue to be the immense sadness, the physical pain of longing and heartbreak. It will be a place of learning, of acceptance, of love everlasting and happiness that you do not need to feel guilty for.

Memories will come as you continue on your journey, things will happen, places will be seen that will bring you back to them like they had never been gone, it will make you want them to be sat next to you and those moments will eventually not be as sad as the early days. I am not sure if you have ever flown, but there is a moment in time when you fly that is so brief you can blink and miss it, when the beautiful orange glow from the sky seems to be one colour but is actually every colour you can imagine. It starts as the most unique purple and if you aren't looking for it you can easily miss it. That's what we find, before we encounter grief, that those first moments of life's events can so easily be dismissed as being insignificant. We take them for granted. We say 'it will happen again', 'they will be there to do that again'. But in just a moment it can be gone and your chance to see it again never happens. Don't ever miss the purple, that's the best bit of all.

Cultural differences

Culturally there is not just one organised grieving process. For me, I have never followed a single path of religion, so it was a swift learning curve to find what might possibly bring comfort. It was only after I found some sort of relief from what may happen beyond our lives, to think there might be a place that he could still exist, that allowed me to carry on and exist myself.

Every religion believes in something beyond. I have looked at many cultures and what they do. When in Vietnam I was told about the funeral and grieving process, one where wailing was not only accepted but expected, a mourning process that went on for years, an expectation, regular appreciation and time to remember the loved ones.

But that was not for me; this was not the English way.

In Jamaica they believe in a nine night ritual, where family return to sing, dance and drink with the rest of the mourners. It is hugely social and a coming together of family and friends. They believe nine nights is enough to allow the soul of someone to pass over, that they may move on from their home peacefully without exacting revenge on those who have crossed them. I could relate to that.

In the Arabic world, and therefore generally Muslim, they believe in the burial of their loved ones as quickly as possible after death. They believe that death, where possible, should be in their own homes, that at the day of judgement they should ask for forgiveness for those violations against people before that of their god.

In Africa, the beliefs vary a huge amount. But the general consensus seems to be that what you do here on earth has less to do with what happens to you in an afterlife. Of course, if you die a murderer, thief or other such unpleasantry you will likely remain a ghost stuck in the unpleasant 'nowhere' place that lies between here and the afterlife. In some parts of Africa there is a custom of removing the dead body not through the door of a house, but through a hole in the wall. A hole is opened up and the body passed feet-first through it; the hole is then quickly closed up again. This is done to prevent the dead from remembering their way back into the house, their feet leaving first so as to ensure that they are pointing away from their previous residence.

Though many of us who have grieved too soon in life can remember wishing so much to be haunted.

In India they have a different view again. Like Africa, the size of the country and diversity of religion gives a variety of traditions and beliefs. Hindus traditionally cremate their dead in order to facilitate the process of reincarnation. After the death of a family member, loved ones are involved in the funeral planning, procession, and burial or cremation of the body. When possible, the cremation is performed on the banks of the Ganges or other sacred rivers, and the ashes are then scattered over the water. The closest relative, typically the eldest son, performs the last rite at the cremation site, lighting the funeral pyre and guaranteeing a release from this world.

Buddhist tradition in India today is centred around a belief in the cycle of suffering and rebirth, driven by karma. The avoidance of unwholesome actions and the focus on positive actions drives the life of the Buddhist, because these actions will plant karmic seeds that will come to fruition later in life, or in a subsequent existence. Buddhism rejects the idea of an eternal soul or any permanent incarnation of self.

Early Buddhists, including the Buddha, followed the Indian tradition of cremation after death and modern Buddhists, including those in the West, have followed suit. Before death, monks will come to the Buddhist home to chant verses to comfort the dying person. These monks will stay with the body after death and continue their chants as the body is being prepared for cremation. I like this idea. There is, for me, something strangely comforting about the sound of chanting; maybe a past life that I will never know about. Having experienced death in its various forms I feel the great importance of comfort.

Jainism is a religion I became interested in through those early months of grief. While it is has a small following compared to other religions it is certainly one to be admired. The religion is centred around a path of non-violence toward all living beings. Distinct to the Jain belief is the refusal to kill animals, insects, or plants for food. They believe that all living things have a soul, that every soul is potentially divine, and that we should therefore treat every living being as we do ourselves, harming none and being kind to everyone. Jains also believe in karma and rebirth, though with some variations from the Buddhist and Hindu traditions. According to Jain belief, karma is divided into the 'destructive', which affects the soul, and the 'non-destructive', which affects the body, with different kinds of karma within each of these categories. The path of the soul is to lead to liberation from the cycle of rebirth and death.

Karma in Jainism, like in Buddhism, is driven by actions in physical life. Depending on one's karma, death can mean rebirth into a physical body on earth, liberation into the highest level of heaven, or enduring suffering in one of the eight hells. Unlike the image of hell in many other major religions, the eight hells become progressively colder as they go down in level, and suffering in this hell is not eternal. Once a soul has endured punishment, it can be reborn to another realm. At the Jain deathbed a mantra is recited and hymns are sung before the body is cremated, typically within twenty-four hours of death. Before cremation, the Jain funeral rites consist of a period of meditation for the peace of the soul, and a sermon and advice to those present. After cremation, the ashes are traditionally scattered in the Ganges or another sacred river. It all seems so complicated, I wondered if a complicated process helps to distract the grief. Though we know that ultimately distraction only prolongs the process to be endured.

Sikhism emphasises a belief in the equality of all humans, and a rejection of discrimination based on caste, creed, and gender. This, I believe, would make it quite difficult to learn life's lessons when we are here, but it is nonetheless one of my favourite ideas - the idea that we are simply equal in all areas of our lives.

In the monotheistic Christian religion, God is a shapeless, timeless, and sightless entity. But Sikh traditions and beliefs are driven by the teachings of ten gurus - from the Sanskrit word meaning teacher, guide or mentor - the first being Guru Nanak. Each guru added to and reinforced the lessons of the previous to create the resulting Sikh religion. At the end of life, an individual is encouraged to recite passages of scripture and focus on God and the divine. After death, the funeral arrangements are made by the family, and include a funeral ceremony followed by a complete reading of the Guru Granth Sahib. The body is traditionally cremated, though other means of disposition may be employed if cremation is not possible. The Sikh funeral ceremony is a celebration of the completion of life, rather than a moment to mourn the passing of the individual, and in this way Sikhism emphasises a resignation to the will of the creator, and sees death as a natural process and an opportunity to reunite the soul with its maker.

That final view is one I learnt to be the most true through my five years of mourning. That death is indeed part of the natural process, and that it gives us a chance to reunite with our maker, whomever that may be.

Of course every country and religion finds a way to garner hope in the depth of their grief, and I have learnt that many of the ideas hold something I could relate to through my own experiences. But my biggest learning is that I feel it is better to respect other people's beliefs regardless of your own. Be quiet as they share, even if you don't believe the same, it is their coping mechanism - their hope when there is nothing left.

Connection and disconnection

People I have met in my research over the past five years have often talked about the feeling of a physical disconnection when someone close to them has died and they are no longer in their presence.

I had a moment that always sticks with me from my journey to the hospital to get to Ben. I did not cry on that journey as I was not aware of what fate was awaiting me, but I can remember an overwhelming feeling as I took a right turn on the road. That right turn is the only part of the journey that stays imprinted in my mind. It has no relevance - I cannot remember the road I was driving on as I just followed the sat nav - I just remember that moment. In that moment I knew life would be different. At the time I just didn't understand why, I believed it was because I would be caring for him to get him back to health.

I have listened to many stories from widows but also friends who have lost parents, or friends who have lost friends, and they all say they knew there was something wrong, it just popped into their minds that there was a problem. When they got to them they were already dead. People try to tell me that souls are not linked and I find it so difficult to believe when I hear so many stories of connection at our most soulful final moments.

Love

Love is a funny thing. We seem to fear the word. We make it bigger than the feelings it promotes and become fearful of our love being unrequited, of saying it too soon, to the wrong person or at a wrong time. It is something that means different things to different people. We can easily block it out and at the same time be overcome by it with no control over where it may take us. But what is it to love?

My parents don't chant the words that they love me, but it has not lessened my love for them, nor the love I have felt from them, because they have never needed to say it. They treat me in such a way that I just know it. They care for me, worry about me, help me on my journey, always have their door open for me and offer hugs in abundance when required. They saw me through my darkest days of grief, and while my suffering continued they put theirs aside. When our final days come, my parents and I will not weep for the unsaid words because we will know that love existed unconditionally. I am always extremely grateful to have been born to parents such as mine.

Some, though, need to hear those words. It got me talking with friends about love. We discussed the respect that you need in yourself to allow love into your heart. One of my favourite sayings is, 'the greatest lesson we will learn is to love and in return allow ourselves to be loved'. Sometimes the latter can be much harder within the stark reality of life. I have personally gone through a period of self-reflection lately, and was brought back to a moment where through my early months of grief, my grandfather held me by each arm, looked me in the eyes and said, 'you have to let people love you'. I recognised what he was trying to tell me, it is only recently I have truly understood that and it is a powerful realisation when you get there. Maybe it is simply when you don't love yourself that you need to be told it by others in order to have reassurance.

So, is it as simple as love follows love?

Love does not need to take its form for lovers alone, it just needs two hearts with kindness, respect, a gentleness of soul towards one another, to then multiply. I have met people along my journey that I have loved and loved because of the people they are, the way they have been with me. Some I have known for just a day and for others for longer, but I would not have spoken words of love to them, it's all too intense, too much for the connection to take it.

So what is it to love? I have concluded that it is unique to each of us. Sometimes it is about the actual word, and sometimes it's about the unsaid words that pass between you, that you wish you could say, to confirm that love exists. For me though, love is simply kindness and with kindness there is love.

Acceptance

I am ok with my own demise, we should all have acceptance of our own mortality. Of course, I would rather not have a painful death, but so often illness is covered by pain relief in this modern world - though not always. When I go, as it is never 'if', this is what I would ask to be read at my funeral; not the words of another person, my words. From my life, that I experienced and know to be something I learnt.

Weep for as long as you need
But do not make the tears, your life
The grief should not define you but turn to love
Take the sadness and turn it into something greater
Greater than I was or you thought you could ever be
Of course life will not be the same, but it does not need to be worse, just different.
It is OK for it to be greater in the end because it will have made my existence worthwhile
When you have wept your tears of sadness and they turn to tears of laughter at the memories we shared, be sure to pass on the love and kindness we shared to strangers that you meet.
Talk of me to those strangers, share the good, laughter, and lessons learnt.
Do not be afraid to say my name, in time it will not hurt, it will be something that brings joy. Go and do the things I cannot do now, do them with love in your heart, carry me with you so I may share your joy. Embrace the impermanence of life, try it all once and say yes often.

Live like tomorrow will not arrive, love like you will never be hurt and when you are hurt accept it as the journey you expect to travel. Finally, thank you, thank you for being part of my journey, I am eternally grateful.

Love Lucy.

I know you must be thinking, 'God, how morbid, where is this even going?' What you learn through all of this, and I guess the reason for this book, is that we do not talk of death. We talk about what will happen in every part of our lives, marriage, kids, house, but never death. Yet death and birth are the only inevitable parts of life, they are the only thing we can be sure of and as birth has already happened if you are reading this book, then your death and the death of others is the only other thing you can be sure of. Therefore grief is inevitable; but regret does not need to be. I will say that again, regret does not need to be.

You do not look at it every day, but plan for it and put the plans away in a safe place so your family do not need to worry about that. Then live your life like those around you and the ones you love could be gone tomorrow. I do not mean weep every time they leave the house. Just embrace them, love them more than you ever thought possible. Do not hold back on love because of some hurt, repressed past you cannot let go of. Let love and belonging swamp you, be vulnerable to it and free to the possibility that hurt will come, that grief will come. Let it be ok that you will never have a regret that you didn't love enough, you didn't allow yourself to be seen, that you lived in a manner that when your final days come you don't say, 'I wish I had.....'

Bitterness

Blame can sit with any person if you wish it to, but the negativity of blame serves no purpose. I have seen blame within grief and it will eat you up, it will not only consume you but your life also. I have seen blame being put onto the person that has died, as that is easy to do. I could have said 'why did you die', 'you must have known', 'you could have gone to the doctors sooner', 'gone back for the results!' Whatever the story. I have seen widows eaten by the blame they have for the person that died. When I think of it it makes me weep, because through his leaving and through his death he has given me everything and so why I should blame him for making me greater than I was yesterday. In your journey of grief, if you feel a negative blame towards them, you must also ask, 'what is the good I must blame them for?' Perhaps the strength, the love, our children, a test on your independence that you survived. Whatever it is, hold onto it, repeat it, say it over and over until the negativity is not even a whisper and you wonder why you had ever uttered them.

You make choices as things will happen in the journey of your life. But it is your choice on how you decide to react to those things. If you expect life to roll along with no challenges, no sadness, that love stays in your life and you will never lose something, you will never grow. You will never grow into adulthood. Look at the greatest people, they have had challenges that are beyond comprehension, but it's because of the choices that they made that they are now who they are. Hiding behind yourself, behind the pain and not sharing it will never allow you to have freedom. Your heart will never be free. If you keep seeking an answer for why it happened then stop, stop right now. You do not need to understand, you just need to know why some have to experience grief at the wrong time and in the wrong circumstances.

I could have said my 'forever' that we had agreed to spend together was not long enough. But it was his 'forever', just not mine. We must understand that 'forever' is only about the now. It is not a planned route where you can say when it ends, as that's not forever and the quicker you understand that, the quicker you will find happiness.

I found that I observe and still observe widows who cannot bear to view others' happiness. They cannot see social media posts that demonstrate people could be living the life they wanted. Do not let bitterness stunt your progress. I see those same widows basking in happiness of new love and new life now. It will come, but the longer bitterness stays with you the further happiness stays away from you too.

Chapter Eight

And finally...

If I knew then what I know now...

After grief you are no longer in a life where you float along with the crowd of people that you once called your friends. You realise the impermanence of it all, a chance to question the world and everyone in it. There is nothing more astonishing than the revelation of realising that the life you had once been leading really was not sustainable for any person with a sense of self worth; it was ok before grief, but after, it was because you knew so much more about your self worth, your own love and loss. The final straw comes and goes so quickly that it is like those people barely existed in your life at all. Equally there are people you will remember for the compassion that they gave you and just as quickly they become strangers in the wind.

My mother was the most astonishing person through my grief. I could not bear people near me so she would just be on the phone for me day after day, three or four times quite often, and just listened, letting me cry. The endurance of my mother going through that, listening to her child cry every day for months, probably nervous to go out in case she wasn't there on the phone for me, will never be forgotten. I do not have enough words of respect and love for her. The astonishing capacity of love that she showed me, taught me we have the capability to give if we so choose to. She showed me that, however bad the world may seem, there is always hope.

Hope is whatever you decide it to be. You can either always hope that there is hope, or you can say hope is hopeless. The journey and the outlook are choices for you to make.

I have strange habits, and I'm not aware of most of them until someone points them out. Ben told me I flex my nose in a rabbit fashion. He had figured out when this was most likely to happen too, but frustratingly I am unable to remember when he said this was. Another sad side effect of grief is the forgotten bits that you can't ask them to remind you of.

My mother informs me that I have always sniffed everything since I was a child. It isn't always just food either: clothes, towels, the list goes on. It is like I am always checking it subconsciously for something toxic. My mother said she was grateful for this habit as it implied an element of cautioned awareness that my mother feared I may not have had. I guess the irony of this is not lost on me.

What happens in grief as we work our way out of the darkness is a fear that you have to overcome. The fear will come in different forms to different people, a fear of leaving the house, a fear of love, relationships, sleep, getting in a car, even talking or crying. The fear will be whatever the grieving person will adopt, but we are not exempt from the side effects of grief.

Grief is something I would never wish again, because I had wished it you see, I had wondered about its depth, how it would feel to lose someone. To feel so deeply I would not be able to fathom those emotions. I have learnt to not wonder what if now, to accept life and the challenges you have, don't imagine the worst as it might just happen, and therefore you can apportion blame onto yourself next time. If I was to write myself a letter that I could send back in time to that fateful day it would be this.

23rd March, 2012

Dear Lucy,

What you are about to go through will take you to the darkest places you have ever been, you will have to muster every part of yourself to make it through the days. You will wish you could be dead. You will dream that you can be with him again. You will be in shock for along time, you won't know it, but you are. Allow yourself to talk nonsense, to waffle on, later on when you look back, there will be messages in those ramblings that you will need later on in your journey. Do not hide from the grief, it's huge I know, but stand and face it, let it consume you and take every part of you. Expect to be burnt to the ashes, you will rise, you will rise stronger than you ever thought possible. You will not remember the person you were last week, that person has gone, be prepared for that. You will lose people who you believe are important today. They won't be tomorrow, you will start to see the world with more clarity once you start to rise. Be prepared for the change, others around you will not be. Be kind in your honesty. You will find honesty so much easier, your tolerance of idiocy will be limited to zero, you will not need to apologise for that.

There will be days when you wish you could be at the funeral, because you know you can't have him back. For a while the grief will drown you, and you will not function, you will need people to feed you and function for you. You will see your true friends, there won't be many. Some will be scared of the grief. They won't want to make it worse for you, they won't want to catch it from you. Watching the pain will be too much for them to bare. Be kind to them in their lack of understanding, help them to know what you need. People will say ridiculous things over the next four years, it is through a lack of understanding, do not blame them for that. Accept it and forgive their thoughtlessness. Do whatever it is that will get you through your days; cry, write to him, watch comedy to attempt to level out the sadness, stare at the ceiling, but remember he is not coming back, he is not coming back and every time you think it you will cry but you will need to, it is sad. Do not drink alcohol to numb the pain, do not accept tablets from the doctor, you are sad, there is no medication that cures that. You have to ride this journey and accept it for what it is. It will be life changing, beyond anything I could even try to explain in writing to you. Expect the unexpected and you will be fine. Find the people who can hear you cry, who will stand by and let you without judgement. Do not cry or grieve in a way that someone else expects you to. Do not fit into someone else's grieving pattern because they can't bear to see you go through your own open and honest grieving approach; it is their problem, not yours. They will need to accept that or move out the way of your journey.

But mostly just be kind to yourself.

Love,

Your friend Lucy.

'Everyone's lives changed that day'. That's what people said, anyway. They shared with me their stories in some attempt to offer comfort. People proposed to their long term partners, they made the break from long and failing relationships that were helping no one. People got their health checked in their hundreds. People told me they couldn't leave the house without telling their loved ones how much they cared. People saw the world differently, it changed them, some for a while and some, like me, forever. That's grief you see, life somehow changes perception so quickly that you are unable to function in the same way as before. When you are not that close to the person who died, the change tends to be semi permanent. It comes and goes and you forget the impermanence of life once again, you forget the importance of being grateful. You continue to exist back in the bubble.

The bubble, as I see it, is a world where you live with no plans, just an existence, thinking that this life will go on forever, with no need to tell or appreciate your loved ones because there is always tomorrow. We need to pop that bubble where we believe that forever is an eternal amount of time, because for some forever is just tomorrow.

Something I need to say, which I have seen too often and read a lot in widows stories of their loss, (I say this gently and with love) but the world has not conspired against you, it is not fighting you.

Something happened that was tragic, sadness beyond words, devastation will subsume you. However, it did not conspire against you, there is a not a person in the sky looking down, trying to make your life a misery. This did not happen to you, or for you, they left this earth and for them the sadness is as great as yours. But life will support the courageous. It's the law of averages, people will be helped when they attempt to put themselves out there, those who say, "well the worst has happened now so I have nothing to lose" become a greater version of themselves than ever had existed. There is a beautifully written book that I recently came across that said something similar, and one of my favourite parts is a mantra the author advises you to have: 'I light up the world by being me'. How true this is, and how extremely powerful.

Make sure the people you are with in your life support your dreams. If those people are negative, tell them, gently. If they are not there for you in a way that you need, tell them gently. They may not be able to support you, but you can walk away with love and understanding. One day your paths may cross and each of your needs will be able to be met. But you become the people you are with, so chose wisely who you want to share your new beginnings with.

Fear of losing someone again is something that I see as a common issue of grief. It's not necessarily that you think they will die, it's not that you believe they will deliberately hurt you. It's just that you are unsure if your heart can deal with the pain of loss again. You understand that, but now that loss can come in so many forms and the risk is one that so many, including myself, find an enlightening journey when you find yourself on that path.

I am stronger. I am so much more after going through this journey, but I would give it all up to have him back That will never end, because memory and love is never ending.

Moving on...

Of course I hurt over my loss, we all do when we lose loved ones. I enclosed myself into a place that was safe, a place I could cope with under the overbearing sadness that the grief gave me. You cannot even imagine opening your heart again in those moments and if you are reading this in your early days of grief, it's ok I wouldn't bother giving it a lot of thought right now.

People who grieve do not need to 'move on' or 'get over it', these are ridiculous comments made by people who need to see that you're doing ok. They need you to be ok with your grief, they need to know that you can cope with it, because they secretly fear that it will be something they will have to go through at some point. They need to feel that there is hope and that it's easier than it looks. You can only love in the moment of right now, but that love lasts forever.

We are programmed to live a certain way. We are expected to have children, do a 9-5 job, have a house and all the other things that we grow up with, whether this makes you happy or not, whether you contribute to society for the better or not, that is the expectation. But what if there is more to life than this? What if we can seek more happiness, more love and more kindness to the world by challenging the norms of our 'acceptable' and shortened explanations of what is important in our lives. Try it in your life, ask yourself what could or might make you happy and simply do that more. Don't do it in the way that is expected, do it in the way that makes you happiest. If your children make you the happiest in your life but you spend more time at work than with your children it is time for a change. If you want to travel the world but never had the means, it is time to find the means.

I have more passion than I have ever had, I am more open to the possibilities of life and death and anything that comes in between than ever before. I do not have a plan until retirement, I will keep changing and evolving, keep saying yes to life. Mostly, I will keep being kind to others and grateful for what I have when I have it, because the rewards are then bountiful. Live like tomorrow may not arrive then you will always live life to its fullest.

I envisaged early on in my grief a tunnel, a tunnel with light at the end of it. At first the light was barely there and I wondered if I could ever reach it, I wondered if I ever would. There was no one at the end that could make that happen except for me, I had to make it happen. I was offered drugs from doctors to help me, but that would serve no purpose other than to blur the light, numb me from the pain, numb me from the darkness that you have to ensure you go through to fully reach the light. My advice is simply say 'Today is a shit day, today I would die if I could, today I don't wish one more day to continue, except to change what time will not allow me to change'.

Whatever it is, be honest. When the day is bad, say it; when it is better than yesterday, say it too. Do not feel guilt for that. You must, through all the darkness, hold onto hope, hope that something will change, eventually you will gain a little strength, just enough to be the instrument of that change. Be in the darkness, it's OK, but know that one day when it's time you will and have to come out of it. Fear of the bright lights of change will be all consuming for many, it causes an anxiety the rest have never suffered. The change and the anxiety is nothing to fear, it will make you stronger than you have ever known, if you face it head on, like the tides of grief. You will not know who you were before and for some you will be glad of that change. I know I was. I was glad I left that person behind, it was who he loved but I sometimes think

I'm loved by many more people in a different way being the person I am now, doing the things that inspire me so that I may then hope to inspire others. If you want the pain to be over, it is natural but it is not the truth of what you need, you need to be immersed into it, to allow yourself to become the best version of yourself that you can be. You will believe that the best version of yourself was when they existed with you on earth but you will discover, on your journey that is might not be the case. The love you had for them will grow and develop into a love that is far greater for the world and everything you want to put into it.

It is so easy to very quickly lose yourself in an addiction, to habits that press in you a self destruct button because it distracts you from the immense pain you are going through. Something I have seen, if you allow those demons to enter, your grief will go on and on, then you are left with more than just grief to deal with. My advice if you are reading this early on in the grief is do not drink, do not allow your body to be addicted to something that will numb you from reality.

There was an article in the paper. It's summary was to say that single people were having the best life. They were not in a couples' bubble, they made an active effort with family and friends. They did not get into the 'comfort' that being a couple can have and therefore went on more adventures and as a result and said 'yes' to life's opportunities.

I can relate to that as when Ben and I settled, while we had a list of adventures we wanted to do, it was a list that would take a lifetime to complete. We got into the safety of each other, the routines. I've been single since losing Ben and while I'm ready to love again I'm also equally aware of how much of life I want to continue to live: spontaneously and with more connections with a multitude of people. It is true that the majority of couples get into a place where they cocoon within themselves. Myself and Ben certainly did, we were best friends that wanted the world to know what we were but didn't tell anyone as we didn't want to ruin it. This is what grief taught me, that only you and your partner will know the connection between you both, good, bad or indifferent. You cannot explain to another person the connection that you have. It is felt, it is not said. So when the person dies, they are the only other person who can understand it. That, in my eyes is the sadness of death, to not look into someone's eyes and you both be able to just know.

What ifs?

So I realised in the end that Ben had asked me, 'Who are you?' He had wanted to know me, understand me, be part of me, my life. I really only heard it after he had died.

I could, of course, dwell on that - on the fact that I didn't hear it when he was alive. The regret, the 'oh I wish I had known how much he saw me, the true me'. That does not heal the sadness though, it does not bring him back. It teaches me to allow myself to be seen now though. I can do that, I can be greater than I was before. To not be that would not only be an insult to his memory but also a slight on myself and my own development. No life should end without something being learnt.

I hope this story and journey may give you even just one piece of inspiration, as that will mean I have taken the memories of two great men and used them for good.

Be inspired.

The title of this book

As the fourth anniversary of Ben's death approached, the number 44 kept presenting itself to me. In the strangest of places, always on the time, on t-shirts, house numbers, roads, car parking tickets, a friend even sent me a picture of the golf cart he was using for the day and, of course, it had the number 44 on the front of it.

Forrest Gump's football t-shirt had 44 on it, the temperature of my sauna... 44°. The list went on and on, every single day. It was coming from every direction. When it first started to present itself I thought it was because it was the year my father was born. So was someone trying to tell me something? I asked after my father's health, he seemed fine. It continued to keep presenting itself day after day though. Then I woke one day and my first thought and memory was that Ben was 44 when he died; I had forgotten this fact, that I had previously thought about and spoken of so many times and to so many people. But '44' seemed a little bland as a title. I had set up a cause called 'Sunshine People' in memory of Ben, which means that each year I do something in his memory and ask that, instead of financial sponsorship, people will sponsor me by a doing an act of kindness for someone else. That they pledge their act of kindness in support of my event, and so ultimately in Ben's memory. Each pledge of kindness like a ray of sunshine - and so the title was found.

http://www.sunshinepeople.org.uk

Acknowledgements

To Alanna (aka Alan) who inspired this book through her incessant questioning of my life, her subsequent fabulous friendship and, in the end, by her reading its content more times than any friend should be expected to.
And to so many other friends (you know who you are) who cheered me on from the sidelines of this journey I call life. I will always be eternally grateful.

Thank you.

Printed in Great
Britain
by Amazon